PRAISE FOR LUCY H... ... W9-BMO-695
AND *GET ORGANIZED IN THE DIGITAL AGE*

"Lucy Hedrick puts technology to work for us! Straight-forward, easy-to-understand information on how to make the most of those gadgets—and our time. I know my 'balancing act'—husband, kids, demanding job—just got easier."

> —Beth C. Hoppe, Director, Science Programs,
> Channel Thirteen, WNET New York

"It's so easy to get organized in this digital age when technology has helped to enhance every aspect of our lives. Lucy Hedrick's book explains the latest cutting-edge hardware and software. As a busy entrepreneur, I know how essential these tools are to manage time and run a business more efficiently."

> —Lillian Vernon, Founder and CEO,
> Lillian Vernon Corporation

"Without making you a 'techno-geek,' this book can empower you to employ information technology to leverage your personal effectiveness."

> —Langdon B. Wheeler, President and Chief
> Investment Officer, Numeric Investors L.P.

"As a longstanding time-and-productivity expert, Hedrick shows an insightful mastery of technology—not an easy task. Even better, she makes it clear and very understandable."

> —Douglas Campbell III, Managing Director,
> TheSuccessCoach.com

continued . . .

"Finally, a book that lays it all out in terms I can understand. After reading *Get Organized in the Digital Age*, I was amazed to realize just how much I rely on technology to run my company. While I travel the world sourcing and meeting with manufacturers, technology allows me to keep in touch and have the knowledge to make quick, informed decisions. Lucy Hedrick's lists of questions helped me focus on what my future needs will be and where to find the answers."

—Patty Nast Canton, President and CEO,
The Nat Nast Company

"Thanks to this book, my PDA is useful. I'm going to tackle digital cameras next. With this guide, it's a cinch."

—Nick Allen, Vice President
and Research Director, Gartner

GET ORGANIZED

IN THE DIGITAL AGE

Use Technology to Save Time,
Simplify Tasks, and Stay Sane
in a High-Speed World

LUCY H. HEDRICK

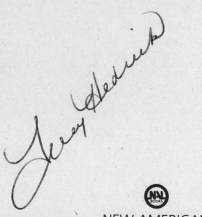

NEW AMERICAN
LIBRARY

New American Library
Published by New American Library, a division of
Penguin Putnam Inc., 375 Hudson Street,
New York, New York 10014, U.S.A.
Penguin Books Ltd, 80 Strand
London WC2R 0RL, England
Penguin Books Australia Ltd, Ringwood,
Victoria, Australia
Penguin Books Canada Ltd, 10 Alcorn Avenue,
Toronto, Ontario, Canada M4V 3B2
Penguin Books (N.Z.) Ltd, 182–190 Wairau Road,
Auckland 10, New Zealand

Penguin Books Ltd, Registered Offices:
Harmondsworth, Middlesex, England

Published by New American Library, a division of Penguin Putnam Inc.

First New American Library Printing, August 2002
10 9 8 7 6 5 4 3 2 1

Library of Congress Cataloging-in-Publication Data
Hedrick, Lucy H.
Get organized in the digital age : use technology to save time, simplify tasks,
and stay sane / Lucy H. Hedrick.
p.   cm.
ISBN 0-451-20651-7 (alk. paper)
1. Time management.   2. Office practice—Automation.   I. Title.
HD69.T54 H442 2002
650.1—dc21   2002019876

Printed in the United States of America
Set in Aldus
Designed by Ginger Legato

PUBLISHER'S NOTE
Accordingly nothing in this book is intended as an express or implied warranty of the
suitability or fitness of any product, service or design. The reader wishing to use a product, service or design discussed in this book should first consult a specialist or professional
to ensure suitability and fitness for the reader's particular lifestyle and environmental
needs. While the author has made every effort to provide accurate telephone numbers
and Internet addresses at the time of publication, neither the publisher nor the author as-
sumes any responsibility for errors, or for changes that occur after publication.

For George

Contents

Acknowledgments   *xi*

Introduction   *1*
A Brief History of Time Management   2
What This Book Is About Today   4
Why Do You Want to Get E-Organized?   6
E-Audit   9

Chapter 1
You Live on the Cutting Edge of Technology   *15*
Trends in Technology Products   16
Mandatory Technology Advisor   17
Lifetime Learning Habits   22
What Do You Want to Do with Technology?   26
The World of Wireless   27
Personal Digital Assistants:
     Do You Need This Technology?   29
       What Kind of PDA Do You Need?   29
Mobile Phones: Do You Need This Technology?   35
       What Kind of Mobile Phone Do You Need?   36
Two-Way Pagers: Do You Need This Technology?   43
       What Kind of Two-Way Pager Do You Need?   44

Combination Devices · 47

Digital Cameras: Do You Need This Technology? · 48

What Kind of Digital Camera Do You Need? · 49

Chapter 2
You Have a System for Processing and Storing Documents · **54**

What to Do with Paper · 55

A Mixed-Paper Recycling Bin · 57

How Long to Save? · 63

Backing Up · 66

Security and Privacy · 69

A Regular Appointment · 74

A Tickler File for Pending Papers · 75

Keeping Track of People · 77

An Electronic Tickler File · 79

Coping with Paper Backlog · 81

Processing Piles of Reading · 82

Reading On-line · 84

Chapter 3
You Have Written Goals and Specific Timetables for Accomplishing Them · **87**

Goal-Setting Requirements · 88

Goals for Every Area of Your Life · 91

The Next Step: Brainstorming · 91

Long-Term Goals · 96

Thoughts Versus Actions · 101

How to Open a Rusty Floodgate · 103

What About the Bites? · 105

Other Handy Lists · 107

Start at the Finish Line · 108

Chapter 4

You Are an Effective Communicator—Adept at Delegating, Optimizing Meetings, and Minimizing Interruptions   110

E-mail Productivity   112
    Lead by Example   116
Telephone Productivity   122
    Consolidating Messages   125
    Speech-Activated Systems   127
Save Time by Delegating   130
    Virtual Assistants   132
Maximize Meetings   133

Chapter 5

You Have a System for Personal Accountability—You Know How to Make Good on Your Good Intentions   137

Getting It Done, Period   138
Accountability Groups   141
Transitioning   142
Ensure Compliance   145
Finding Focus in a Fog   146
The Challenge to Disconnect   147
Ride the Wave!   150

Index   151

Acknowledgments

This book would not have been possible without extremely helpful insights from Charles Asmar, Bill Bausch, Drew Bisset, Scott Brenner, Jeff Carlson, Debra Feldman, Brad Fisher, Susan Laliberté, Abby Marks-Beale, Allen O'Farrell, Lee Paine, Chris Pankratz, Roz Pollock, Caren Schwartz, Jan Wallen, Steve White, Stuart Welkovich, and Midé Wilkey.

I am further indebted to George Handley, Tod Hedrick, Joanne Hoppe, Julie Jansen, Sheri Koones, Louise Lague, Anne Rockwell, Betsy Schenkel, and Karen Watt, for propping me up and cheering me on. Without their emotional support I wouldn't have been able to scale the rock face. And my devoted agent, Denise Marcil, and inspired editor, Hilary Ross, helped to make the journey a memorable one.

And finally, Susie Haubenstock, Joanne Kabak, and Jane Pollak were tireless editors, commiserators, and friends, and they made me accountable. Hats off and huge hugs to all!

*S*teven L., age thirty, *lives with the constant feeling of being overwhelmed, of always being behind, both at work and at home. A successful salesman for an international company, he loves his job but worries that he's stretched so thin things are slipping through the cracks and he will lose clients without timely follow-up. Steven also suspects that he's not making the best use of the technology tools that his company provides.*

Also stretched and stressed to the limit is Lorraine D., age forty-eight, *an interior decorator. She is trying to keep several enormous decorating assignments on time and on budget and is stymied about how she and her staff can better manage these projects, as well as handle their many vendors and contractors.*

Aaron F., age thirty-nine, *is an award-winning artist who realizes that his technology-enabled colleagues are surpassing his sales and commissions by leaps and bounds. He fears that unless he updates his computer and other office equipment and pursues marketing opportunities on the World Wide Web, he will experience diminishing exposure and revenue. With limited financial resources, Aaron doesn't know how and where to begin.*

* * *

Each of these individuals could benefit from getting organized, but more specifically, from getting "e-organized." Thanks to the timesaving electronic devices that are available today, it is possible to save time, reduce steps, keep track of details, and simplify our lives—the by-product of which is *reduced stress*. And who doesn't want that?

But there are so many electronic gadgets out there, and more are arriving every nanosecond: two-way radios, handheld organizers, MP3 (a Motion Picture Experts Group standard for audio compression) players, digital cameras, so-called smart keyboards—for example, the AlphaSmart 3000 (www.alphasmart.com)—digital highlighters, mobile phones that transmit photos, and so forth. The technology industry itself refers to the rapid changes as the tsunami—which aptly describes this man-made tidal wave—of upgrades, new products, and more and more information. How does one deal with it all?

A Brief History of Time Management

Let's take a quick moment to review whence we've come. Time management has been around for a while. I first heard about it as a child in the 1950s when "efficiency experts" like Frank Gilbreth (*Cheaper by the Dozen*) and his fellow engineers were doing "time and motion" studies. They tried to reduce and simplify the number of steps that it took to manufacture a product.

In the 1970s, pioneers like Alan Lakein (*How to Get Control of Your Time and Your Life*) and Edwin Bliss (*Getting Things Done*) applied time-management principles to business executives. Then in 1978, Stephanie Winston burst on the scene with her groundbreaking *Getting Or-*

ganized: The Easy Way to Put Your Life in Order, which made the *New York Times* bestseller list and told us how to organize our things, as well as how to plan our time.

In 1985 the National Association of Professional Organizers (www.napo.net, 512-206-0151) was founded, and there followed a groundswell of organization books, including my own *Five Days to an Organized Life* in 1990. The tools I and others recommended for getting organized were all paper-based—pocket calendars, pocket notebooks, file folders, and so on. Hundreds of thousands of the converted marched around with their Filofaxes, Day-Timers, Day Runners, and Franklin Planners.

Enter the IT (information technology) revolution! Manufacturers design and build computers that are faster and faster with more and more storage capacity, and now with miniaturization, they are smaller and smaller. Software engineers design and build timesaving programs that help us do our work. The computers produce information in large quantities, requiring our time to analyze it, refine it, absorb it, report on it, and so on. And now the Internet also provides enormous amounts of data, but this, too, takes time to acquire, analyze, and use.

To help us manage everything, we now have personal digital assistants (PDAs), such as Palm Inc.'s extremely popular Palm Handhelds, and the next generation of wireless Internet PDAs. We have cell phones and pagers and voice messaging. We have speech-recognition software and even "smart houses." Soon, no doubt, we'll have "smart offices." All these tools bring us increased connectivity and more data faster, which results in an infinite increase in information and plain old work within a finite workday.

In 1991, Juliet B. Schor published a fascinating study *The Overworked American: The Unexpected Decline of*

Leisure, in which she demonstrated how in every new technological phase since before the Civil War, Americans have invented timesaving appliances—the cotton gin, the automobile, the washing machine, the computer, and so on—but with all that time saved, Americans have consistently filled their lives with more work. And just as before, despite the most profound "revolution" in our history, technological advancements spur our perennial hue and cry, "I have no time!"

At the same time, journalists and commentators give us regular columns and editorials that cry for "a balanced life." To help us find the balance, we can choose from a plethora of wilderness travel experiences designed to get us "away from it all," as well as from an extensive menu of relaxation treatments available from day spas. So while the techno-junkies consume all the gadgets, they are also demanding recreation, quality time with friends and loved ones, and some peace and quiet . . . in short, *reduced stress.*

What This Book Is About Today

Get Organized in the Digital Age is a book about productivity, about going from point A to point B, quickly and smoothly—with an emphasis on *simplicity*. The book's basic premise is that technology equals *access*, not deluge. You will be encouraged to embrace technology as an organizing tool, which when used correctly increases productivity and therefore results in more time for fun . . . which is, after all, why we want to get organized—so we can get our work done and *have fun*. Yes, it is possible to make choices that will get rid of the mind-set of having too much to do, of so often feeling overwhelmed. This book will show you these alternatives and the specific benefits of choosing them.

Get Organized in the Digital Age will help you get your arms around the tsunami—the IT revolution—in a manageable way, one day at a time. You will learn how to do research, get advice, and make decisions with a minimum of fuss. Just as important as knowing what electronic organizing tools exist is knowing how to assess their time-saving benefits. Furthermore, while a by-product of the IT revolution can be information overload, *Get Organized in the Digital Age* promises antidotes and strategies for coping.

As I crisscross the United States and talk to thousands of men and women about their time challenges, I observe that organized, time-efficient people share five characteristics, or what I prefer to call *lifestyle choices*:

1. They are on the cutting edge of technology—they use technology to save time.
2. They have a system for processing and storing documents (on paper as well as in electronic form).
3. They have written goals and specific timetables for accomplishing them.
4. They are effective communicators—adept at delegating, optimizing meetings, and minimizing interruptions.
5. They have a system for personal accountability— they know how to make good on their good intentions.

I devote a full chapter to each of these five characteristics, and you will be shown electronic solutions to the problems that waste your time. We all have twenty-four hours every day, but we have different financial resources and varying energy levels. Our values—what we like—are also different, so I will make several suggestions. The choices are yours, but if you follow my suggestions, you will be more *productive*—you will get your work done more efficiently so you can *stop working, relax, and have fun.*

Why Do You Want to Get E-Organized?

As an author and entrepreneur, I have tried to stay current with technology, to simplify my business life as much as possible, and to indulge in an exciting and fun-filled personal life. Before I undertook this project, however, I conducted an "e-audit" with my own personal "e-coach." And I confess to you that we found lots of room for improvement. At the end of this introduction is the e-audit that we performed. You, too, will be invited to examine your e-life and identify where you suspect that you might need an upgrade.

No one can dispute that life is moving very fast these days, nor that change is a constant. An intelligent individual recognizes the need to surround himself with experts—a good lawyer, a reputable accountant, a primary physician, and so on—people who study their subjects full-time and who are equipped, and indeed licensed, to advise the rest of us who do not have such qualifications. If you want to save time, simplify your life, and be more productive in today's world, you also need a technology advisor—someone whose full-time job it is to stay current on computers, telephones, the Internet, and all manner of electronic devices. I call mine my e-coach because he teaches me as well as solves my computer problems. If you work for a large company, you may be lucky enough to have tech-support staff to answer your e-queries, but I doubt it's available to you evenings and weekends at home. Furthermore, you may only stay aware of changes affecting your work systems. Every individual or family needs its own tech support. (How to find this support is discussed later.)

It is now possible to live your whole life on the Internet. In fact, a computer systems manager from Dallas did this in a yearlong trial as DotComGuy, so we know it can be done. For example, you can conduct your financial affairs on-line, run your business on-line, communicate with friends and family on-line, order everything you need on-line, and have most items and services delivered to you. No one has to talk to anyone face-to-face.

What is possible may not necessarily be desirable, however. Do you really *want* to lock yourself away from the rest of the world? I doubt it, although I'm sure we occasionally have days when it's a fantasy worth contemplating. A consummate extrovert, I need to see people every single day, so I would never be a good candidate for a DotComGal opportunity.

A young man said to me recently, "These days, if you're not confused, you're not in business." All those in our conversational group laughed, but inwardly I winced at the remark. As a time-management expert, I know that confused does not equal productive. Therefore, I fear his quip reflects a mind-set that will sabotage his efforts.

In contrast, I prefer the philosophy of successful artist and entrepreneur Jane Pollak (www.janepollak.com), who says, "I'm a lifetime learner. Some days I learn more than others, and some days I feel like I'm a 'freshman' again, but I'm permanently enrolled in 'e-college.' "

I propose we adopt a new attitude toward technology.

Fear and avoidance, panic attacks, or eyes glazing over must be kept at bay, and I will show you how. Our mantras must be, "I will step up to the technology plate, I will acquire knowledge, and I will use it." In fact, my purpose in writing this book is to enroll my readers in e-college so that they will find satisfaction, joy, and humor in all that technology offers on the journey toward becoming more productive.

When I first began researching and outlining this book, I had major panic attacks. I felt as if information on technology products and services was coming at me as hard and fast as water through a fire hose. How am I going to deal with this? I wondered. Where do I start, and more important, where do I stop?

Then I took several deep breaths, secured some quiet time, and "ate the elephant one bite at a time" (see chapter 3). I listed what I could realistically talk about in less than two hundred pages and thought about the best order in which to present my current knowledge and what information I would acquire through research. Then I sat down to tackle that elephant, one bite at a time.

When I address an audience about e-organization, I frequently begin by asking, "How many people here drive a car?" Without exception, everyone raises his hand. It's a life necessity—everyone has to drive. Even if you live in a city, someday you're going to want to come out to the countryside, and that usually involves driving.

Some people take to driving like the proverbial duck to water. A few practice sessions in deserted parking lots with a licensed driver, and they're eager and ready to pass their driver's license test and take to the road. Others are more cautious—they sign up for formal driving lessons and require more sessions around the parking lot and quiet streets. Some acquire the hand-eye-foot coordination more slowly than others. Nevertheless, we all learn to drive.

And what did that first driver's license mean when you were fifteen or sixteen or whatever age? It meant *freedom*—freedom from parents and freedom to see your friends and go places. I remember it was an exhilarating feeling.

Acquiring skills at *saving time and being organized* with electronic devices is similar to learning how to drive. Some people have natural-born techno-savvy, and others, myself included, require more tutoring and practice. But we all can learn—in our own way, one step at a time.

And the big payoff from getting e-organized is just as with driving: greater freedom—freedom from forgetting things, from losing things—in short, freedom from chaos. And can't you just imagine how exhilarating that will be?

How about you? What do you want to simplify? To organize? To be more productive? Take a moment to respond to the following situations honestly. This is *your* e-audit, and it is step one of living an e-organized life.

E-AUDIT

Answer yes or no to the following statements:

1. When I can't find the answer using my software's "Help" feature, I make use of free, on-line technical support, but I also have a technology advisor, "geek," or e-coach who replies to my calls or e-mails promptly.
2. I keep all my passwords, PIN codes, software registration numbers, and other key codes in a secret, secure place.

3. I have a hard-copy file of all my tech device invoices, warranties, and service agreements.
4. I regularly visit on-line technology stores and information Web sites.
5. I regularly visit computer and electronic stores in person to learn what's new.
6. I seek out, collect, implement, and share timesaving shortcuts for the software I use regularly.
7. I carry electronically my contacts—my address book—with me at all times.
8. I carry electronically my calendar and to-do list with me at all times.
9. I keep track of income and expenses electronically on a daily basis as I incur them.
10. My PDA is Web-enabled, or I know how to use my cell phone or attachable wireless modem to access the Internet.
11. I know how to use my PDA to send and receive e-mails and text messages, and how to get specific information from the Web, such as stock quotes, news, movie listings, and the like.
12. I can make a call with my cell phone from almost anywhere.
13. I have all the contacts I would ever need to reach by phone stored in my cell phone so I do not have to attempt to memorize phone numbers, call directory assistance, or look the numbers up on another device.
14. I use my cell phone as a wireless modem to access the Internet using my laptop or PDA (or I have a wireless modem built into my laptop or PDA).

15. I know how to use 100 percent of the features on my cell phone.
16. I have the fastest, high-speed, broadband Web access that is available in my geographical area and that I can afford.
17. I actually know how fast my connection is.
18. I am familiar with security issues on the Internet and therefore have a firewall for my high-speed broadband Internet connection and do not leave my computer "connected" when I am not using it to access the Internet.
19. I know how to "clean" my browser caches, history, and TEMPORARY INTERNET FILES folder to prevent anyone from going to my computer and looking at or figuring out what I was doing on the Internet.
20. I am efficient at using on-line search engines to locate specific products or to search in general categories.
21. I pay my bills on-line.
22. I manage my investment accounts on-line.
23. I use e-mail for 95 percent of my correspondence.
24. I make use of my e-mail software's capabilities for sending group e-mails.
25. The only "junk" e-mail I receive is that for which I've given permission.
26. I know how to use the BCC (blind carbon copy) function of my e-mail program so that I can e-mail a group of people without them having to scroll through a large list of names just to get to the message.
27. I know how to use the filter functions of my e-mail to sort incoming mail to designated folders or to delete it.

28. I know how to create and use customized "signatures" for my e-mail.

29. I (or my technology advisor) perform regular maintenance on my computer.

30. I can send a fax right from my computer. I don't have to get out of my chair.

31. My computer probably has enough storage space to accommodate my needs for the next three years.

32. I back up my most important files regularly.

33. I store my most important files on an off-site, password-protected server.

34. I have a sturdy antivirus program that even checks compressed (or zipped) files and e-mail and continuously monitors my machine for viruses.

35. My printer is fast and capable of printing the most sophisticated graphics that I encounter on the Internet.

36. I have a "Web-cam" or a camera I use on the Internet.

37. My computer's processor is fast enough for the work I perform, and I can upgrade it if I want to without replacing my whole computer.

38. I have and know how to use a scanner and how to scan photographic slides and negatives.

39. I have a good video or sound card in my computer (or both).

40. I am comfortable hooking up a printer, scanner, digital camera, or other device using a USB (universal serial bus), Parallel Port, or infrared capabilities on my computer.

41. I know what a URL (uniform resource locator) is.

42. I know how to find the "available resources" on my computer and my PDA.

43. If, suddenly, I can't connect to the Internet, I know where to start looking for the problem.
44. I know how to track changes in word-processed documents.

Count your *yes* responses. How did you score?

Gartner Group, the technology research company based in Stamford, Connecticut, has coined some helpful words to describe the speed with which companies and individuals adopt new technologies: pioneers, mainstream, and followers. If you answered yes to more than thirty statements in the e-audit, you can be termed a pioneer—that is, one who jumps in and tries new tools as soon as they're available. If you answered yes to twenty to thirty questions, you are mainstream—that is, you probably wait for later versions of a new product before giving it a try. If you agreed with fewer than twenty statements, it suggests that you are probably a follower—someone who waits for new products to become fully established before buying in.

No matter where you are on the road to e-organization, the journey will be less confusing and frustrating if you enroll in e-college. I also promise the excursion will be invigorating and fun. Let's get started.

Chapter 1

You Live on the Cutting Edge of Technology

*F*rank and Anne E. *want to join the digital age, but they haven't a clue how to begin. They both use computers at work—Frank as a real estate agent and Anne as a librarian—but they want to bring technology into their home also. Frank wants a mobile device so he can keep in touch while he's out showing houses to prospective buyers, and Anne suspects they could save a lot of time with some kind of electronic calendar. "Where do we start?" she asks.*

Jane K. needs a technology coach. She wants desperately to do all her banking and bill paying for her home-based business as well as for her family on-line, but she's totally frustrated and confused. The bank sent Jane the software to install, but something's amiss. She says, "I want to hire someone who will get it all set up and show me how to do it."

Kirk O. bought one of the first handheld organizers, and he loves how it has helped him e-organize his calendar and address book. An ad space salesman on the go, he now feels left behind because he's unable to access his e-mail or use the Internet with this handheld. Does he need a new device, or can he add an external modem? And what about service plans? What does he need to know to shop intelligently?

What do Frank, Anne, Jane, and Kirk have in common? Each wants to become more proficient with technology. They know that by learning more and improving their technology skills, they will increase their productivity. Why should one choose to be on the *cutting edge* of technology? For the undeniable reason that technology saves time—much more time than we can save with manual or paper systems. The universal example most everyone can relate to is when computers replaced typewriters. Can anyone believe that we used to be slaves to Wite-Out and the endless retyping of drafts?

Yes, as I myself often say—usually following a computer crash, an e-mail never received, or a dropped cell-phone call—technology is only good when it works. But for the vast majority of time, it does work and it saves us huge amounts of time. Machines and systems do break down, but we can plan for that eventuality and minimize lost time in fixing or replacing them.

Trends in Technology Products

Electronic products move through a product cycle, just like most other products. The first version arrives in the marketplace, and it's often large and expensive and has flaws in its operations. Subsequent versions eliminate the bugs, make improvements, and are often smaller and less costly. And yes, manufacturers have certainly planned for built-in obsolescence. Just as we watched the arrival and disappearance of the eight-track audio player, we have also seen the departure of IBM's original DOS (disk operating system), 5¼-inch floppy disks, and gigantic mainframes.

Timesaving gadgets like PDAs, mobile phones, and digital cameras are mirroring these trends. Thanks to advances in miniaturization, computers, telephones, and cameras got smaller and faster, and they are able to store larger amounts of data. In addition, products are "bundling" functions. Consider, for example, Canon's Multipass all-in-one device, which combines a printer, scanner, copier, and fax machine into one unit (http://consumer.usa.canon.com/index.shtml) and Samsung's Uproar phone that combines an MP3 music player and a digital phone (www.samsungusa.com). You will observe the product cycle again and again as a lifetime learner about technology.

Mandatory Technology Advisor

As I stated in the introduction, every individual or family needs a technology advisor—someone whose full-time job it is to stay current on computers, telephones, the Internet, and all manner of electronic devices—who's available to help when disaster strikes. He or she should also be available by e-mail when you have a question that's not urgent. My on-call "geek"—he doesn't object to the label—lives minutes away, which is purely coincidence, but also obviously convenient. What's more, he bills me in quarter hours, which saves me money and probably helps increase his revenue because I consult him frequently. If my computer or Palm organizer needs a quick adjustment, *it's a better use of my time* to page Allen, suspecting that he can find the solution in less than fifteen minutes, than for me to waste time struggling with manuals or help screens.

When I canvassed two dozen business associates on how and where they found their tech support for home or for integrating work and home, 75 percent said they found their advisors through personal referrals. "I ask my friends whom they use," says Meredith M., an attorney who relies heavily on her geek to keep networked and e-organized with her husband, two kids in junior high, and part-time nanny.

And when you think about it, isn't that the way most of us find our most trusted advisors (traditionally, attorneys, accountants, and physicians)? "Referrals from friends save a lot of time," remarked Tom J., a systems engineer who, one would think, would be able to provide his own tech support. But for Tom, it's about *the best use of his time*. "When I'm home from my job in the evening and on weekends, I want to spend my time with my family and out of doors. The best use of my time is *not* solving my family's PC-networking problems or reprogramming my wife's cell phone. So we pay Robin to do it."

With referrals from friends or close associates, the time-saving value is in the reference-checking that's already been done. Friends usually give honest evaluations that highlight why they're pleased with their advisors and any less-than-ideal conditions that you need to be aware of.

Some of the services you might expect from your advisor, which you would pay for, include

- Hardware and software add-ons, upgrades, and repairs
- Adult and youth tutoring on software products and the Internet
- Setting up multiple computers and servers for home business operations and family use

- Installing a network to share faster Internet connections and higher-quality printers at home
- Building a business or personal computer from scratch or purchasing a brand-name machine
- Designing and implementing a business or personal Web site

Advice on choosing ISPs (Internet service providers), computers, hardware, and software is usually free, within reason.

If you meet someone, for example at a social gathering, who says she provides computer support and advice, or you respond to an advertisement, ask the following questions:

- What are your qualifications?
- What services do you provide?
- What are some examples of tech problems that you've solved recently?
- When are you available?
- How does one contact you?
- What is your response time?
- What do you charge, and how do you bill (some consultants travel with credit-card-charging capabilities for in-time payment)?
- May I have the names of three local references?

My friend Steven L., a graphic designer, successfully used these questions with his PhotoShop 6.0 instructor at the local continuing education branch. Steven thought the instructor, who purported to provide tech support for small businesses, was knowledgeable and an effective teacher, but he needed to inquire further about the depth and breadth of the man's knowledge. Now a steady and satisfied client, Steven says, "Sometimes continuing-ed centers with computer software teachers are good places to find tech support locally."

With so much information available, I believe it's also timesaving, as well as money-saving, to have a *telecommunications* advisor for wired and wireless telephone services—a "T-coach," if you will. More about this concept follows in the discussion on mobile telephones.

For those who prefer on-line solutions or who need the capability to ask questions anytime anywhere, tech support is very much available on the Web at no cost or at very low cost. Five sites offering *free* answers to your tech questions are

- Allexperts, www.allexperts.com
- CNET Help, www.help.com
- Helptalk Online, www.helptalk.com
- PC Show and Tell is free for thirty days, www.pcshowandtell.com
- Trouble Shooters, Inc., http://cruisewithme.com/help

An important caveat about all these sites is that you can pose your questions anytime, anywhere, but answers can take a while to return. Further, while PC Show and Tell provides free answers, you must download and install a viewer—that is, software that permits the consultant at the other end to "see" your computer screen.

In addition, there are Web sites that "bid" to answer your questions:

- EPeople Help Desk, www.epeople.com
- Expertcity Inc., www.expertcity.com

In each case, you decide what, or if, you're willing to pay, and fees start at just a few dollars. For those who crave a human voice, Expertcity offers telephone advice.

Subscription services are yet another way to go:

- Ask Dr. Tech, www.askdrtech.com
- MyHelpDesk, www.myhelpdesk.com
- Tech Know-How, www.techknow-how.com

PC Show and Tell, under free tech support, also invites users to consider subscription options. For example, thirty dollars per year buys you a variety of extras, including unlimited access to forty thousand software tutorials and tips. And like Expertcity, MyHelpDesk also provides phone support. Ask Dr. Tech provides a thirty-day trial and even has PC insurance and theft and vandalism coverage for its premium members.

As everyone knows, Web sites come and go. All the above on-line tech support sites were located by searching for the phrase "on-line tech support" on any of the major Internet search engines, such as Yahoo (www.yahoo.com), Excite (www.excite.com), Go (www.go.com), or Google (www.google.com).

Finally, it's very possible that, when you buy your hardware or software, you are entitled to on-line tech support from the manufacturer, often for free for a limited duration. Or perhaps you purchased a service contract. If you are permitted to use, or have bought, this service, you should e-mail the manufacturer or call its toll-free number as your first source of support. (I'm assuming you have not been able to find answers to your questions by looking under the "Help" feature of your software.)

I frequently hear users complain that toll-free help lines can be incredibly frustrating. Many software companies, after asking you many questions to which you must reply by voice or numeric keypad, try to divert you to their on-line support when what you really need is a human voice. These delays are especially annoying if you're accustomed to an immediate voice response to your tech questions at work. Hence, the proliferation of small businesses offering in-person or live-phone computer support.

Last, but not least, if your budget is tight, bartering for technology advice was practiced by several families that I interviewed. "Geeks need to eat," says Sharon J., who, along with her roommates, provides home-made Italian dinners for Vernon in exchange for computer and networking troubleshooting. I found others who swapped help-desk support for haircuts, pet care, and car servicing.

Again, the question is, *What's the best use of your time?* If the ideal help standard is 24/7 (twenty-four hours a day, seven days a week) in real time, how much are you willing to pay? Or how much of your own valuable time are you willing to devote to finding tech support that is free or costs less?

Lifetime Learning Habits

To stand on the cutting edge of technology, you must practice several learning behaviors so that they become *habits*. Remember, you are a lifetime learner permanently enrolled in e-college. The result of cultivating these habits will be improved e-literacy:

- Read, on-line and off-.
- View and try demos.
- Shop, but don't buy . . . yet.
- Ask, ask, ask.
- Share tips with colleagues.

As I confessed to you at the beginning of this chapter, I could easily go blind and crazy reading all that is written about technology today. Instead, I confine my information sources to one daily newspaper (with above-average technology coverage), one computer magazine in hard copy, and one on-line subscription that regularly e-mails me technology news briefs. That's more than enough for my busy schedule.

When professional speaker Rebecca Morgan talks to audiences about technology, she advises, "Go to a large bookstore and peruse several computer magazines. Choose just one that's at your level, and buy a subscription. Then commit to extracting at least one idea per issue to leverage your time."

To locate sources of technology news briefs on-line, I searched for the phrase "on-line technology news." Favorites, which I bookmarked, include:

- Bloomberg Online: Technology News, (www.bloomberg.com/bbn.technology.html)
- CNET.com, (http://news.com.com/2001-12.0.html?-tag=hd_ts)
- IDG.net, (www.idg.net)

Another knowledge-enhancing habit to embrace is to continue your "classroom" education, either in person or on-line. Continuing-ed classes through your public school system or at local colleges are providing entry-level software courses right on up through advanced levels. For those who prefer studying at home on-line, check out:

- PC Show and Tell (www.pcshowandtell.com), which offers multimedia tutorials on more than one hundred different software applications, including

Microsoft Word, Excel, and the Lotus and Corel Suites.

- SmartPlanet (www.zdnet.com/smartplanet/), which charges a monthly fee of $15.95 that buys you access to many areas of learning, including computing and technology.

- A superb directory of on-line instruction can be found at World Wide Learn (www.worldwide-learn.com). Here you'll find hundreds of on-line courses, degree programs, certificates, professional continuing education, and learning resources in numerous subject areas offered by educational institutions, companies, and individuals from all over the world. Technology courses are easy to find.

Web sites that provide on-line learning for senior citizens (but there are no age restrictions) are attracting a huge following due to their gentle approach and conspicuous hand-holding. For example, if you are really new to the Internet, but determined to learn the basics and more, you can't do better than courses offered at:

- Internet for Beginners (www.netforbeginners.about.com)
- Internet 101 (www.internet101.org)
- Learn the Net (www.learnthenet.com)

Many on-line learning sites provide opportunities to cultivate another learning habit—viewing and trying demos. True, these Web sites are clever marketing tools: give the customer a free sample, and she'll probably buy more. But there's no obligation, and FreeSkills.com doesn't even require a user registration. So there's no fear of unwanted e-mail or other intrusions. Short of the most timesaving way to get a recommendation—through a trusted friend—jumping in and trying a course yourself is the next best thing.

Retail computer, electronics, or office supply stores can be intimidating at first and are not always known for knowledgeable salespeople, but if you view a quick visit to one of them as a casual trip to a museum to check out what's new, they seem less onerous. Shopping, just to see the latest gadgets or their software, is also part of e-learning.

Alison P., a mortgage broker and mother of three, describes her "window shopping" trips to learn about mobile phones: "I just fit in one trip to a phone or electronics store on each of three consecutive Saturday mornings, along with my usual errands," she says. "I had researched the different models, as well as the various service plans, on-line at CNET.com, and I had talked to my friends. But personally, I needed to feel and touch and hold different mobile phones to see what model made the most sense for me."

Lifetime learners are curious people by nature and are always asking questions. "Tell me where you found that." "What was that shortcut again?" "Why do you like your PDA?" Get in the habit of asking people about their e-preferences, their e-tricks, and their e-organization. I strike up these conversations with people all the time, and I find that people love to talk about what they like and don't like about their gadgets. Furthermore, I've instituted technology-tips-sharing opportunities with several groups I belong to. We share our e-tips in person when we convene off-line, and take turns passing software shortcuts via e-mail in between meetings. Each person provides just one suggestion so there's plenty of time to practice and make it a habit. Yes, sometimes the advice is not new to everyone, but I have never participated in one of these exchanges without everyone receiving one or more timesaving ideas.

Before readers cry, "Help! I don't have the time!" over my recommendations—read the trade press, view and try demos, window-shop, ask questions, and share your shortcuts—let me stress that you are encouraged to practice these behaviors a little at a time. Schedule them into your electronic calendar—incorporate them into your life. Again, people who stand on the cutting edge of technology are not necessarily geeks, but they are definitely lifetime learners.

What Do You Want to Do with Technology?

It's very important that you know the answer to this question before you can get e-organized. Do you remember when you set out to buy your first computer, and the salesperson or your geek or your best friend asked, "Well, what do you want to do with your computer?" Today, do you want to do wireless or mobile, or do you just want to send e-mail greeting cards? Do you want to bring your large and cumbersome and bulky Rolodex into a CRM (customer relationship management) software program or do you just want to access the Web and send e-mail? What would you like to simplify? What would you like to e-organize?

The recurring fantasies of technology are portability, interoperability, and affordability. *Portability*, of course, means that you can easily carry the device with you any-where, anytime. That may be a fantasy for many devices, especially desktop computers, which are heavy and need to be plugged in to a power source. However, the overall trend to miniaturize is bringing more memory, more storage capacity, and more function to smaller and smaller appliances. Witness the proliferation of PDAs. And the whole wireless phenomenon has also contributed to greater portability.

Interoperability means that you can use your devices with everyone else's. This, too, can be fantasy, because different products use different operating systems that make it difficult for them to "talk" to each other. However, as more companies get together to subscribe to universal standards, some of these barriers are breaking down. Companies have begun investing in the competitive advantages of software rather than focusing on unique systems.

Affordability is an individual matter entirely, because what's affordable to one person may be entirely out of reach to another. But recall a typical product cycle: As winning products catch on in the marketplace and subsequent versions are improved, the prices usually come down, making products that were previously inaccessible attainable for more buyers.

So, assuming you, too, long to be e-organized with affordable products, some of which are portable and interoperable, what do you want to accomplish with these tools?

The World of Wireless

The rest of this chapter is devoted to several portable electronic tools—PDAs, mobile phones, pagers, combination devices, and digital cameras—all of which require batteries or need to be "charged" (or both) in order to operate them. Many of these gadgets can and should be "synchronized" with your principal computer. Some devices, like mobile phones and pagers, call for service plans. (Some phones or pagers can be Web-enabled, providing you with access to the Internet through that device, which can be part of one service plan or an additional service plan.) All the possibilities are dizzying, and the lingo is confusing. However, by knowing *what you want to do* with the device and by practicing e-literacy habits, you will learn how to evaluate products to determine if they can help you be more productive.

I assume every reader owns, or regularly uses, a computer with Internet access and either owns (or is thinking seriously about buying) a PDA, a mobile phone or pager, and a digital camera. Perhaps you own early versions of these tools, and you are on the cusp of upgrading to products with more timesaving features.

As you learn about tools that are new to you, you will also learn how to assess their *productivity* value to you. (If you want to buy a gadget because you want it, regardless of its timesaving properties, that's an entirely different decision.) The first question you have to pose regarding a new tool is, Do you need this technology? For example, you might ask, Will this device reduce paper waste? Will it make things move more smoothly in your life? Will it condense many steps into a simpler process? If you answer yes, then you must determine: What type—that is, what features and functions—will be best for you?

Personal Digital Assistants: Do You Need This Technology?

For me, my PDA (personal digital assistant) is a boon to my productivity because, first and foremost, wherever I go I carry my electronic calendar, address book, and to-do list in the pocket of my jacket. The ability to look up a client's or friend's phone number or e-mail address, look up a restaurant's phone number, or remember a book title as I stop into a bookstore, right then and there, saves me a great deal of time. I never have to make an excuse like: "Sorry, my Rolodex is at home" or "My calendar's at the office—I'll have to call you."

In addition, as a sole proprietor of a small business, I keep track of my business expenses and tax deductions as I incur them. Using the Pocket Quicken (www.landware.com) application, I can synchronize all of my daily entries with Quicken (www.quicken.com) on my desktop. This makes for accurate and timely invoicing of my retainer clients every month and tremendously lightens my work as I prepare my annual tax returns.

Another feature of the latest PDA versions is the ability to "beam" a phone number, a to-do item or a memo to another PDA through infrared connections. All of this saves huge amounts of time.

What Kind of PDA Do You Need?

There are many PDA products on the market today, and a good number of them come with Internet connectivity. (Albeit, the pages look different from the ones you view on your larger desktop or laptop computer screens.) Furthermore, more products, more software, and more peripherals are emerging every day. Whenever I want to research any product remotely connected to business or technology, I always start on the Internet at:

- BuyerZone.com (www.buyerzone.com)
- CNET.com (www.cnet.com)
- Outpost.com (www.outpost.com)
- Computers4sure.com (www.computers4sure.com)

Most of these sites allow you to create your own comparison chart. It's as easy as selecting up to five products and clicking on the COMPARE button.

It's important to note that the lingo for PDAs is confusing. They're also called handhelds and palmtop organizers and personal organizers, and the more expensive varieties with more memory and features are called pocket PCs. It gets down to what operating system the unit has:

- The Palm OS from Palm, Inc., runs the Palm PDA, as well as many other devices for which Palm has licensed their system (such as the Visor from Handspring).
- Pocket PC OS from Microsoft runs, for the most part, the more sophisticated and expensive PDAs from Casio, Compaq, Hewlett-Packard, and others.

To decide what you want to accomplish with your PDA, ask yourself:

- Is small size most important, or do I want a PDA large enough to have an actual keyboard?
- Am I comfortable learning the shorthand "graffiti" required by some units?
- Is it necessary for me to see the letters as I write them on the device's screen?
- Do I need an internal modem for e-mailing or

browsing, or just the capability to add an external one later if I choose to?

- Do I need a color screen, or will monochrome do?
- Do I need the ability to turn my PDA into a digital camera?
- How do I prefer to keep my PDA charged: replace batteries (hopefully rechargeable) frequently, use longer-lasting lithium batteries, or let the unit recharge itself when resting in its cradle?
- Do I need enough disk space and memory to do word processing and spreadsheet applications, or do I primarily need to keep track of my contacts, calendar, to-do list, and expenses?
- Do I want my PDA to play music, such as MP3 files?
- Do I need a *continuous* syncing feature so that my PDA automatically saves a copy of any appointment, contact, or document from my hard drive?
- What other software can I add?
- As a tradeoff to many, many features, how tolerant am I to "crashes"?
- Do I need a reader program to display entire books on my PDA?
- How much do I want to spend?

This is a very long list and not intended to overwhelm you, but rather to act as a guide. Remember your *lifetime learning habits*. Considering what PDA to buy or to upgrade to is very difficult without talking to users and touching and feeling several different models.

With so-called "Net-ready" PDAs, you must pay monthly service charges, often through your cell phone carrier, to access the Internet. And as I said earlier, it's essential to realize that the wireless Internet is very different from the one you reach on your desktop or laptop computer. First of all, wireless Internet speeds are slower than the most simple dial-up modems on home computers. Second, what you see is most often a limited number of text-only Web pages—weather, stock quotes, sports scores—that are stored on your Web service company's closed servers. Or if your service company promises that you can reach *any* Web page using your PDA, what you see are pages that have been digitally compressed before transmission. In other words, wireless Web pages have to be reconfigured, one way or another, for the wireless Web because PDA screens are so small. In this regard, an important service-related question to ask yourself is, Do I need integrated wireless Web access for lots of browsing or will I just be doing occasional e-mail?

In addition to BuyerZone, Outpost, CNET, and Computers4sure, here are additional on-line sources of information on PDAs:

- www.handango.com
- www.pdastreet.com
- www.memoware.com
- www.palm.com/products/compatible.html

I also recommend the free PDA Productivity Guides, which I receive via e-mail once a month from www.mobile-generation.com.

Again, in choosing to buy a PDA, ask yourself, "What do I want to do?" The more hardware, software, and peripherals you buy, the more you're going to spend out of pocket, and why own what you're not going to use? For example, if your need is to have the members of your family share your calendar and electronic address book, you don't need a PDA to do that. Web-based data-sharing services are available for free from sites such as:

- Yahoo (http://calendar.yahoo.com)
- Protonic.com (www.protonic.com)
- FusionOne (www.fusionone.com)

Additional PDA caveats include the following:

- Make certain your choice of PDA has enough memory to do what you want it to do.
- Regularly synchronize your PDA with your desktop computer, which must have its own backup system. (More about *backing up* in chapter 2.)
- Choose a PDA with a warranty that provides a loaner device if yours needs repair.

One of the many benefits of the newest technology devices, especially PDAs, is their ability to be customized for *your* life. Yes, even beyond loading *your* calendar, *your* address book, and *your* to-do list, you can install software especially designed for handhelds that keeps the information *you need* at your fingertips. For example, Jeff Carlson (www.necoffee.com), author of *Palm Organizers Visual Quickstart Guide*, swears by the following free or low-cost e-organizing programs, which he has installed on his PDA:

- AvantGo (www.avantgo.com) Web Client takes information from the Web and corporate intranets, and gives you up-to-date information.
- BrainForest Mobile Edition (www.aportis.com) is a tool for outlining and mind mapping.
- Documents to Go (www.dataviz.com) allows you to use Word and Excel files on your PDA.

- HackMaster (www.daggerware.com) is a system extender for all sorts of tweaks and add-ons.
- HourzPro (www.zoskware.com) is excellent for tracking your time, expenses, and mileage.
- Launch 'Em (www.synsolutions.com) is an application launcher and a sequel to LaunchPad.
- Vindigo (www.vindigo.com) provides events, restaurants, and directions in major cities.

These applications, or at least their demos, are free from Download.com (http://download.cnet.com). Be sure to determine for which operating system they were developed. To find additional programs for the Palm OS and Windows CE, visit Handago.com (www.handango.com). For Palm OS only, try PalmGearHQ (www.palmgear.com). A very helpful site for PDA software reviews in general is www.pdajd.com.

"I think more people should try reading a novel on their PDAs," Jeff Carlson adds. "I love having some reading material when I travel that doesn't take up extra room in my bag." While very few people would want to read something that long on such a small format, free document reader applications are available. For example:

- CspotRun (www.32768.com/bill/palmos/-cspotrun)
- Iambic reader (www.iambic.com)
- ISilo (www.isilo.com)

When you realize how many activities PDAs are capable of, you could legitimately ask if these pocket-size gizmos are going to replace our desktop computers. I believe it will be a while before our desktops go the way of the dinosaurs. However, with the trend of software applications being delivered more and more over the Internet—as exemplified by all the free stuff listed above—I also believe that these compact devices will grow more powerful and ubiquitous. As I say this, I am acutely aware that *right now* the only thing that is big enough and fast enough to keep pace with the innovations on the Internet is the desktop (or laptop) computer.

To sum up, PDAs are exciting productivity tools, but there is a learning curve attached to using one. (For transitioning to technology devices, see chapter 5.) Remember, the key question is, *What do you want to accomplish with your PDA that you can't do without one?* If you will save time by having your calendar, address book, to-do list, and other functions always with you, then it's time to purchase one or upgrade the one you have.

Mobile Phones: Do You Need This Technology?

Simon W. lives by his cell phone. "I'm never home, and I'm never in my office," he says with a laugh. A network integrator for a large state university, he and his team of six roam the campus in golf carts as troubleshooters for computing and networking problems in every office and building. "I'm 'mobile tech support' and couldn't survive without my cell. I try to answer every call, although I'm often using speakerphone while I'm following wires in a ceiling or under desks. I've assigned different ring tones to different caller groups. When the university president calls, he gets me after the first ring."

At another extreme, some users reserve their phones for minimal call-outs and emergencies only. "I use it only if I'm going to be late for an appointment, need directions, that kind of thing," says Susan R., a CPA. "I'm responsive to my clients, but I don't need to be accessible every minute. The only people who are permitted to call in on my cell are my husband and my childcare."

What about you? Would you save time if you could make phone calls when you're away from your office or home but not near a pay phone? Would you feel safer if you or your loved ones were able to place a call in case of an emergency?

What Kind of Mobile Phone Do You Need?

It should come as no surprise that, when you decide to buy your first (or a new and better) cell phone, you ask yourself, "What do I want to do with my mobile device?" Proponents of cell phones say they provide the ability to call anyone at anytime (well, not quite, but wireless phones offer more portability than the phone on your kitchen wall), while two-way pager advocates argue that these devices let you send and receive e-mail anytime, anywhere (well, again, not quite, but with more portability than with your desktop computer). What product you choose will have a lot to do with the service plan you select, but there are some basic hardware considerations, too. For cell phones, ask yourself:

- Do I need dual band or dual mode (for digital and analog networks) to distinguish between different frequencies and various cell phone technologies? (Digital phones can be equipped with Internet and message features. Analog technology is older, but service is available throughout the United States.)

- Are there tone, vibrate, and on-screen indicators that alert me to incoming calls or missed calls?
- Do my needs require triband, which can be used worldwide?
- Can I turn off the annoying key tone (the tone that sounds aloud whenever a key is pressed)?
- Is there an equipment protection plan in case of theft or loss of my phone?
- How many phone numbers will I need to store?
- Do I need to organize my stored contacts into groups?
- How many numbers would I like to program for speed-dialing?
- Do I need a "Net-ready" cell phone to access Web sites, or just the ability to receive and send short text messages?
- How many display lines of text do I need?
- Do I need the ability to send "picture greetings"?
- Do I need a calendar in my phone?
- Do I need to be able to connect my phone to my laptop (with a laptop modem card that is cellular capable), turning it into a wireless modem?
- Do I need a combination cell phone and two-way radio?
- Do I need a built-in clock, alarm, or stopwatch?
- Do I need the ability to store a certain number of incoming and outgoing calls?
- Do I need downloadable ring tones?
- Do I need hands-free accessories?
- How much battery time and standby time do I need?
- Do I need the ability to play games on my phone?
- How much do I want to spend?

Searching for the phrase "cell phone comparisons" turns up the following Web sites, which are especially helpful for on-line research:

- www.eshop.com
- http://equip.zdnet.com
- www.4cellphones.com
- www.lowermybills.com
- www.point.com

All my cell-phone-using colleagues cautioned me against shopping *only* on-line. "Web sites contain all the hype," Christine M., a Web site developer, warns. "Nevertheless, they can be great places to find the best deals after you've zeroed in on your top two model choices.

"Even though many mobile service plans give you a phone or a heavily discounted one when you sign up, there's no substitute for trying out phones or pagers in person," she continued. "You've got to touch them, hold them, push the buttons, listen and see how the different models feel." I agree.

During several months I canvassed many of my friends—geeks and nongeeks—who are cell-phone users. Once again, when I sought their counsel regarding what service plan to buy, they universally asked, "Where and how will you use it?" Just like computers and their handheld offspring, mobile phone usage determines the choice within your price limitations. John Castenada, a consultant with Communications Business Services, Inc., in Ardsley, New York (www.cbstelecom.com), says, "Ask yourself if you plan to use your phone in your immediate local calling area, in your regional calling area, nationwide, or worldwide. In addition to whom you will be calling and from where, know when you will place the bulk of your cell-phone calls. The most important, and obvious, tenet is that you want low-cost calls for the area you will call most often."

Your next productivity decision regarding your cell-phone service is what *service* features do you need?

- Call waiting
- Call forwarding
- Caller ID
- Three-way conference calling
- Detailed billing
- Voice mail
- Voice mail with paging
- Text messaging
- E-mail forwarding
- Wireless Internet service
- Voice command

It's possible to sign up for cell phone service when you purchase your cell phone, but a credit check must take place first. A few examples from the plethora of service-plan options include:

- A low-end usage plan, say, ten dollars per month plus the cost of each call
- A flat monthly rate with "buckets of minutes" included
- Prepaid options, but you are paying higher per-minute calling charges
- A family plan that links two or more phones to one group of minutes

Most service plans require that you sign a contract for at least one year. This is controversial among consumers because competition between plan providers is fierce, and you may want to switch when you learn of better terms. A key question to ask is, Will you switch me without charge to another low-cost plan provided by this company if my wireless usage changes during the course of the contract?

Cell phones are convenient and save time but are in no way as reliable as our "wired" or land-line phones. Every user I talked to complained of service interruptions and "dead zones." They also complained of unexpected roaming and long-distance charges on their bills. Yet they argue in favor of phones over pagers "because everyone has a phone."

"Users cannot expect the same service as they get from a wired phone," Drew Bisset, a telecommunications consultant, maintains. "Overloaded, congested networks— even the weather—can affect service.

"There's still controversy over cell-phone transmission sites, and there's a lack of available spectrum, or frequency bands," he explains.

The optimists insist that soon there will be truly seamless service across the United States, but right now, no single provider can cover the entire country. The good news is that the Universal Wireless Communications Consortium is working on standardizing incompatible cell-phone technologies, and the industry is negotiating with the FCC (Federal Communications Commission) for more spectrum. Does a solution lie with satellite phones? Not yet, say most analysts, due to the high cost of phones and the necessity for "land stations" to process calls.

More helpful information on productivity from cell-phone service plans can be found at the following sites, located by typing "cellular-service plans" into an Internet search engine:

- www.point.com
- www.buyerzone.com
- www.cnet.com
- www.cellmania.com
- www.wirelessadvisor.com

Several of these sites offer the added benefit of inviting you to type in your zip code for the plans serving your geographic area. Then you are permitted a side-by-side comparison of up to five plans.

However, if you don't have time to research cellular service plans yourself (or wired long-distance services, for that matter), or if you find the plethora of plans and features simply too dizzying, a telecommunications consultant— your T-coach—can tell you what's available in your area and explain the different options to you. Their service to you is free; these consultants are *brokers*, and they are compensated by the service companies to whom they bring customers. (The type of telecommunications consultants I'm talking about are *not* resellers—persons who buy a million minutes deeply discounted and then resell them at a less-than-retail price.) The best ones can represent as many as twenty providers (depending on what's available in your area), and they can find you the best deals for personal or residential service, as well as business applications.

Another value of telecommunications consultants is in the clout they have with service plans. Top consultants bring thousands of prequalified, good-credit-risk customers to the service carriers, so if you're having a billing problem or customer-service issue, consultants have access to top personnel and go to bat for you.

Where do you find a reputable consultant? The ones I

know I've met through business and social networking. Most operate regionally, so you can usually find them through your local Chamber of Commerce. A testimonial from a friend or acquaintance is the best reference.

New cell-phone features and service-plan add-ons make news every week. While preparing this chapter, I learned about new battery packs that contain rechargeable solar cells (www.SNPower.com), as well as Simulring service (www.simulring.com), with which your friends and family can call just one local phone number, but it rings on up to three lines. Whichever line is picked up first—your home, office, or cell—gets the call. No more calling all around to find you. And from Blink.com (www.blink.com), mobile users can import their desktop computer bookmarks to their Web-enabled phones (or other handheld wireless devices). No more grumbling about having to type in URLs on miniature keypads.

An important caveat if you receive free content—stock quotes, news, weather—with your wireless messaging—these services are also accepting advertising, which means you are going to receive ads unless you *pay* not to. So what you thought was going to be free may not be *totally* free after all.

As much as I promote the expertise and timesaving value of consultants, they can't know everything. It's up to you to stay current on new products, as well as service enhancements, and then tell your advisor when you want additional services.

Finally, will owning or upgrading a cell phone allow you to enhance your productivity, or will it bring further interruptions into your already disrupted life? Will voice mail, call forwarding, and other cell-phone service-plan features reduce the amount of time you have to spend at the office and grant you more personal time? Or is it a tool that you view as appropriate for emergencies only? Know the answers to these questions before you dive in.

Two-Way Pagers: Do You Need This Technology?

"We wouldn't survive without our two-way pagers," insists Marilyn F., who with her husband, Jack, runs a busy commercial production company. Parents of three children in school, they keep in touch in and out of their studio with e-mail on the go.

"During a commercial shoot, there are no cell phones allowed, but I know I'm needed when my pager vibrates. Since we got our two-way pagers, we haven't missed a kid pickup yet," Marilyn says.

There are many types of pagers—one-way numeric, one-way alphanumeric, two-way alphanumeric, and satellite or global messaging pagers, to name a few—and many of these are used in the workplace to save time and to be in constant communication with other workers. However, for living an e-organized life, I will discuss the more elaborate two-way pagers—sometimes called PICs (personal interactive communicators), which offer e-mail messaging on the go. Popular wireless pagers such as Motorola's Timeport (http://motorola.com/MIMS/MSPG/Products/Two-way/timeport_p935/) and Research in Motion's (RIM) BlackBerry (http://www.blackberry.net/), while considered handhelds, come with keyboards—a distinct advantage over PDAs that require the user to learn a special script. Advocates insist pagers are more reliable than cell phones and point to their antivirus firewalls and security, as well as the greater privacy of e-mail. Furthermore, pager e-mail beats cell-phone e-mail, they insist, due to larger screens that can hold more text. However, before the uninitiated assume that pagers are perfection, be forewarned that there are limitations. Just as with cell phones, one must pay for two-way pager *service*, which may or may not include Web access, and in truth, there can be annoying outages.

For the most part, two-way pagers store more e-mail addresses—more than two thousand in some models—than the most robust cell phones. Pagers can also allow you to receive your e-mail from the office—that is, to interface with office software systems. Moreover, like some PDAs, they are capable of the infrared transfer of data known as beaming. For example, BlackBerry pager users can now receive wireless calendar updates in addition to address book entries. Finally, though more expensive than cell phones, two-way pagers tend to have a much longer battery life. (Actually, in standby mode, they use about the same amount of juice, but it takes more power to encode and decode voice signals than it does to work with simple text characters.)

What Kind of Two-Way Pager Do You Need?

In choosing what two-way pager to buy, some of the features you will need to consider are:

- Does it have password protection?
- Does it have built-in reply messages and shortcuts to make my response time as quick as possible?
- Does it have memory backup, which stores messages when I'm out of reach, my battery is dead, or the

pager is turned off, and then delivers them automatically when I'm back in range? (This is often called automatic e-mail retrieval.)

- How many messages can the pager hold? (Most pagers hold from eight to twenty.)
- Are there tone, vibrate, and on-screen indicators that I have a message?
- Does it offer PC connectivity and desktop synchronization via a docking or charging cradle?
- Is it PC compatible and upgradeable?
- Does it have a lighted keyboard?
- Does its display screen have backlighting?
- How many lines of text would I like to see on the screen? (Typically there are from four to twenty.)
- Does it have an alarm system that I can set to remind me of appointments and events?
- Does it have a rechargeable lithium battery?
- What size microprocessor does it have?
- How much memory does it have?
- If I'm going to access the Internet with my pager, is it info and data receptive?
- How much am I willing to spend?

More information on two-way pagers can be found by searching the Internet under "two-way pager comparisons," or at these Web sites:

- www.actpage.com
- www.buyerzone.com
- www.eshop.com
- www.gadgetguru.com

Like wireless phones, the paging service determines the type and features of the pager. It's usually best to determine your paging service first, before buying a pager. Know that all paging-service features are not available in all areas. Questions you need to ask regarding two-way pager services include:

- Can I send and receive text messages?
- Does it confirm message delivery?
- Does the service offer Internet access to my existing e-mail account?
- Does the service offer fax access?
- Is there an equipment protection plan in case of theft or loss of my pager?
- Does the service offer Web browsing and Web information on demand? (With some services, you can get customized subscriptions to news and sports updates, stock quotes, and other information.)
- Is there a toll-free message service so friends and family can page me from any location without incurring long-distance charges?
- Can I check my pager messages by phone when I don't have my pager or I'm outside the pager's range?
- Is there automatic roaming so the pager's range follows me wherever I travel?
- How much am I willing to spend every month?

Again, with so many service options and so much information available, I believe it's timesaving as well as economical to have a telecommunications advisor for two-way pager service. As Jack F., the busy commercial producer and father of three, points out, "The service plans keep changing, and new providers enter the market all the time. At the end of my contract, should I switch to a new, lower-cost plan? Are the carriers reliable? Our telecom consultant studies this arena full-time and gives us sound advice."

But more to the point, in *your* life, will the ability to send and receive e-mail anytime, from anywhere, make you more *productive* or will it become a constant interruption, preventing you from getting your work done quickly and accurately? People have complained to me about the volume of e-mail they receive. If you were able to access and process some of it while you're on the go— away from office or home—would that mean you would have less e-mail to deal with when you return? Or conversely, are you setting up an unrealistic expectation that you respond to all e-mail immediately, that is, in *real time*? (Strategies for managing e-mail volume are discussed at length in chapter 4.)

Combination Devices

Just to muddy the electronic waters even more, wireless devices are beginning to intermarry. For example, consider Motorola's Accompli 009 (www.motorola.com/accompli009), which combines a mobile phone, PDA, two-way pager, and Internet connectivity in a handheld device. Or there's LG's device, the LGI-3000W (http://www.lginfocomm.com/home/LGI3000W_phone.asp), which marries a flip-style Internet-enabled cell phone with a PDA that holds up to two thousand entries in the phone book and up to one thousand in the calendar. And now Kyocera has licensed the Palm operating system to produce their Smartphone (www.kyocera.com). Kodak has also joined the more-is-better bandwagon with its Kodak MC3, an MP3 player, digital camera, and digital video camera (www.kodak.com/go/mc3).

We have seen the strategy of bundling many features into one device before. Remember when television manufacturers began to produce combination TV and VCRs? The first versions were not flawless. The VCRs tended to malfunction first, so buyers were stuck with a working television and a broken VCR. But true to the product cycle, the manufacturers worked out the bugs, and now many more combination models are available—and earning high consumer praise—many with the addition of a DVD (digital video disc) player.

Is more necessarily better? Only you—and your lifestyle and your pocketbook—can decide. The most important question is, *Will one of these all-in-one devices save you time and help you to be more productive?*

The point is you must do your research: Check consumer reviews on-line, and ask your friends why they swear by their all-in-ones. And where *productivity* is concerned, if you take notes on your PDA while talking on your cell phone, it probably doesn't make sense for you to combine all these functions (unless you don't mind using a peripheral ear piece). So again, when considering a new technology product, ask yourself, *What do I want to accomplish with this product?*

Digital Cameras: Do You Need This Technology?

No doubt about it—digital cameras are becoming almost as popular as cell phones, pagers, and PDAs. When they first appeared these cameras were very expensive, but prices have come down, and picture quality continues to improve. But do they save time? Absolutely.

"You don't have to wait to get your photos back from the developer," says Rita, newly married to Terry and happily sharing their wedding photos on the Internet with friends and relatives who were unable to attend the ceremony. An enthusiastic convert, she adds, "With my digital camera, I can preview a picture before I take it, and I can instantly view a just-shot photo and delete the rejects. I can import them into my computer for fine-tuning and print them in color on my own printer. Plus, there's no more expense for film or processing."

Lee Paine, award-winning photographer and columnist for Southern Connecticut Newspapers, has led me to her favorite sources for learning about digitals. Current reviews of digital cameras can be found in issues of *Popular Photography* and *Consumer Reports* magazines, as well as on the Web at:

- B & H (www.bhphotovideo.com)
- The Camera Zone (www.thecamerazone.com)
- Computers4sure.com (www.computers4sure.com)

Again, Computers4sure.com allows you to create your own product comparison chart.

What Kind of Digital Camera Do You Need?
After you've decided that a digital camera will enhance your productivity, there are issues that you need to consider as you go to buy a camera:

- Will the camera be compatible with my computer system?
- Does the camera use a memory card or a floppy disk to store its photos? Which of these will work best for me?

- How many megapixels (picture elements) do I require to get the kind of pictures I want?
- Do I prefer a point-and-shoot autofocus or manual overrides for focus and shutter speed?
- Do I want a video component for taking thirty- to ninety-second videos that can also be downloaded to a computer?
- How much do I want to spend?

In addition, you must think about the following as you look at cameras:

- What are the size, weight, and shape of the camera?
- How durable is the camera? Is it made of plastic or metal?
- What is the design of the menu system and how do I access it?
- From the viewfinder, can I see my picture in detail or is it fuzzy?
- Do I require a zoom lens?
- Do I need a panorama mode?
- Is there a rechargeable battery?
- Do I require my digital camera to double as a Web camera?
- Do I want spot metering—that is, the ability to take individual light readings for different portions of my picture?
- Do I want a built-in flash with multiple functions?
- Can I use the flash from my 35 mm camera system as an auxiliary for the digital?

An alternative to sending digital photos over the Internet is a photo-sharing Web site to which you can direct your friends and family. For example, check out:

- ClubPhoto.com (www.clubphoto.com)
- DotPhoto (www.dotphoto.com)
- Visto (www.visto.com)

A comprehensive listing of photo-sharing sites, with consumer reviews, can be found at *http://dir.yahoo.com/ Business_and_Economy/Shopping_and_Services/Communication_and_Information_Management/Internet_and _World_Wide_Web/Personal_Information_Management/ Photo_Albums/*.

Most of these sites let you add captions and edit your images, but if you want to create albums and Web graphics, these inexpensive software programs are excellent image-editing tools:

- Microsoft Picture It (www.microsoft.com)
- Ulead PhotoImpact (www.imira.com)
- Adobe PhotoDeluxe (www.adobe.com)

Be aware that you do not need a digital camera to share your pictures over the Internet. Many retail film developers will provide you with a compact disc of your photos, as well as the usual prints and negatives. However, with a traditional camera you incur the costs of film and processing.

My friend Allen O'Farrell provides tech support for businesses, as well as individuals, and some of his more esoteric assignments include elaborate computer installations on very large oceangoing sailboats. He explained what an important and timesaving role his digital camera plays in these installations: "When I have completed an installation, I photograph everything—all the wires, all the connections, all the settings—with my digital camera. Back in my office, I download these photos onto my computer into a simple [Microsoft] Word document and then label everything. Later, if a skipper is having computer trouble, I open his Word doc with labeled photographs and can usually diagnose and fix the problem over the phone."

If you are Internet-savvy, you're probably wondering if the labeled photos could be stored on a remote server so the sailboat captain could retrieve them himself. Assuming he has the time and desire to acquire that knowledge and skill, the answer is, definitely. More about on-line storage in chapter 2.

Few of us have installations as complicated as those on a large sailboat, but think of what you could photograph and label to save time and be more e-organized. Many homeowners are using their digitals to photograph and share instantaneously the day-to-day progress of new construction.

I recently heard of Erin A. and her mother, Laura, who are organizing Erin's wedding over the Internet. From bridesmaids' dress choices to bouquet designs to wedding cake selection, Erin, who lives on the opposite coast from her mother, has asked for comments and suggestions while sharing instant photos for every decision.

Susan and Mike N., relocating from New Jersey to Seattle, were able to keep in touch via e-mail with digital photos while Susan did the house hunting. She showed Mike and her two children at home not only the outsides and insides of potential homes to buy but also the neighborhood schools, parks, and downtown retail sections. "I was the only one free to travel to Seattle," Susan recalls, "but what house to buy was a family decision."

Before you leap to the conclusion that a digital camera is the answer to all your prayers, know that there are interoperability issues. You can't download from every camera to every computer. You need a program that is compatible with the digital system you are using. Also, photos stored on your hard drive can take up a lot of space. Moreover, digital cameras don't stand up to travel as well as traditional ones. They are more sensitive to heat, moisture, extreme cold, and rough handling.

Again, as a consumer your first question is, *What problems can I solve with my camera?* And second, will the timesaving features and enhancements to my personal productivity justify the extra cost of a digital? Remember, the manufacturers and their inventors are conspiring to bring new cameras with new features—some of which are easier to use and save time—to the marketplace every day. If you are a *lifetime learner* (read, on-line and off-; view and try demos; shop, but don't buy . . . yet; ask, ask, ask; and share tips with colleagues), you will be better prepared to make the right choices.

Obviously, I can't cover all of the technology gadgets. Just to stay current on PDAs, mobile phones and pagers, and digital cameras has been a full-time job—a challenging one and, I hasten to add, an exhilarating one. Read up, tune in, and ask for advice. By practicing my lifetime learning habits, you, too, will become proficient at evaluating the different devices to determine if they will contribute to your e-organization.

Chapter 2

You Have a System for Processing and Storing Documents

*V*ickie L. *is a self-confessed "piler." "I've got piles for everything—financial stuff, papers relating to my kids, file folders for my bookkeeping clients, newspaper clippings for the trips I'm going to take 'someday,' estimates from general contractors to build a family room addition. I've got so many piles, I can't move!" she cries.*

Laura V., *an executive coach, had left her home office to run a quick errand when a sudden, violent thunderstorm came up. She returned home to find the power was out. When it was restored, she learned the horrible truth—she had lost everything on her computer's hard drive. Her tech advisor is trying to restore what he can, but Laura is determined to install a suitable backup system to prevent future disasters.*

Paul S. *realizes that he wastes a great deal of time looking for things—papers for a client meeting, electronic documents on his computer, people's contact information for his mortgage broker business. "I put things away," he says, "but I can never find them again. This afternoon I tried to find a phone number in a drawer full of hundreds of business cards. Help!"*

* * *

In our digital age, it is necessary to keep track not only of paper documents, but of electronic ones, as well. However, despite the predictions of the prognosticators, paper has not yet disappeared. In fact, many observers insist it rains down on us with increasing force and volume. I was amused to read in my local newspaper that my town has been investigating storage alternatives for its piles of paperwork. It appears that the amount of public records is bursting the seams of town hall. Many individuals also tell me that they're running out of space in their paper file drawers and on their computer hard drives.

One thing is certain for both electronic and hard copies: Deciding what to toss and what to keep, and then where to store what you retain, is a constant challenge—for individuals, for companies, and even for municipalities. This chapter will guide you through the steps for processing and organizing your papers—hard copies and electronic.

Judy Scherer, editor in chief of *Competitive Edge Magazine* (www.compedgemag.com), notes that "people spend too much time *processing* and not enough time *performing* their job." I agree. So what can be done to reduce your paper processing time?

What to Do with Paper

Stephanie Winston, organizing guru and author of *Getting Organized: The Easy Way to Put Your Life in Order*, gave us the acronym TRAF, which refers to the four things that can be done with a piece of paper—hard copy or electronic:

T = Toss; throw away, or delete as much as you can
R = Refer; forward the document to another person

A = Act; complete the task now
F = File; put away the document for safekeeping

"Sure, sure," says Mike L., owner of a large retail store and father of four, "that's common sense. I know all that. But why am I continually surrounded by piles of paper? And why can't I find what I'm looking for?"

Mike's complaint is very common. It has been said that clutter—or piles of paper—is postponed decision making. In any case, Mike has his piles because he has not yet tossed, referred, acted on, or filed those papers. But the solution to the paper avalanche is more than these four choices. You have to have a system for dealing with your paper so it doesn't pile up.

There are four parts to an effective, timesaving document system:

- A mixed-paper, and an electronic, recycling bin
- A regular appointment with yourself to process documents
- A paper "tickler file"
- An electronic calendar or CRM (customer relationship management) software program

The first way to reduce your paper processing time is to curtail the amount you receive. And by the way, if you wish to substantially reduce the amount of junk mail you receive, send a letter to: Direct Mail Association, P.O. Box 9008, Farmingdale, NY 11735-9008. Include your name and *be patient*. It takes up to six months before the full effects will be felt. And if you're passionate about reducing paper in the world, visit New American Dream (http://www.newdream.org/junkmail/step1.html).

Electronically speaking, another hue and cry I hear

often is, "I don't need to be copied on every e-mail document!" This is mostly a workplace complaint, but families with several computers that are networked and who resent the proliferation of e-jokes taking up space in everybody's e-mail box have joined the chorus. Strategies for reducing the flood of e-mail are discussed in chapter 4, but suffice it to say that minimizing the papers that are referred to you is a communications issue. Ask the perpetrators to refrain.

A Mixed-Paper Recycling Bin

When you go through your inbox at work or examine your snail mail at home, sit or stand next to your recycling bin and throw away as much as possible. Abby Marks-Beale, owner of the Reading Edge (www.the-reading-edge.com) in Wallingford, Connecticut, teaches people how to read faster. She says, "If it has a bulk rate stamp on it, let it go." I would add another category: if the envelope reads, "You have been preapproved for . . ." I know I don't need any more credit cards.

After tossing, it's often necessary to sort, or refer, documents for other members of your family. For households with more than a single resident, professional organizer Susan Laliberté, Systems Plus, recommends, "Every family member should have their own inbox, and children (and caregivers picking them up after school) should learn to put those teacher notes and permission slips into Mom's or Dad's inbox."

Acting on a document as soon as you receive it is ideal, but often unrealistic. "If I had nothing else to do all day, I could just sit here and process paper," complains Sarah W., a financial analyst and single mother who receives volumes of investment reports at work and the usual flyers, permission slips, and report cards from her three elementary-school-aged children at home. Sarah sorts her mail by category—pages to read, bills to pay, documents to file—so she can process a lot of each category in one sitting. She has also become adept at reading investment reports and processing paper in "snatches of time," such as while commuting by train to work or while waiting for medical appointments.

Sarah's comment above—"If I had nothing else to do all day"—is crucial. Staying on top of paper and electronic documents is essential also, but to enhance productivity, you must continually ask yourself, *"What is the best use of my time?"* Paper tasks can be high, medium, or low priorities for you. What's vital is that you get to your high priorities first. (More about setting priorities in chapter 5.) This is why Sarah sorts her papers first and then processes a low-priority category of paper quickly.

"Like with dairy products, the 'expiration date' is critical," Sarah cautions. "I make sure I highlight right on the form the due date or deadline for all of my kids' school papers."

Which brings us to *F* for file. Your most important consideration is where to file a document so that you can find it again quickly—in your paper file cabinet or on your hard drive. How you title your file folder (paper or electronic) is a very subjective decision. If your teenager has a fender bender, will you look for your automobile insurance policy in a folder called CAR INSURANCE or among all your insurance folders (car, home, business, health, and so forth) under INSURANCE—CAR? It's up to you. Similarly, if you keep an electronic list or spreadsheet of investments you've made for your children's higher education, do you store them in an electronic folder labeled COLLEGE, which contains the summaries for John, Morgan, and Charles as separate documents? Or do you store JOHN'S COLLEGE MONEY, MORGAN'S COLLEGE MONEY, and CHARLES'S COLLEGE MONEY in an alphabetical list under MY DOCUMENTS? Again, the choice is yours. The assumption is that you will go in and out of these documents as you add new information and form the habit of always finding them in the same place. This is a productive system.

The only materials you need for a paper filing system are a file drawer, or several, and file folders that you label and then file alphabetically.

A sample of paper files that most everyone should keep includes:

- Automobile(s)
- Bank account information
- Bills to be paid
- Canceled checks, if you still use them
- Credit card(s)
- Eyeglass or contact lens prescriptions
- Home improvements
- Income tax returns
- Insurance
- Investment records
- Medical insurance claims
- Mortgage information
- Pet records
- Receipts for income tax deductions
- School records
- Warranties
- Will and estate planning documents

Because we live in the digital age, it should come as no surprise that software has been created to help you manage paper. I'm not referring to document imaging and elaborate database management, both of which you may be accustomed to at work. I mean paper management software for individuals and families. Consider, for example, the Taming the Paper Tiger Software Kit produced by Barbara Hemphill (www.productivityconsultants.com). The kit, for single user or network use, comes with a multimedia tutorial, preprinted file folder tabs and a user's guide. The software is a database that resides on your computer and that tells you when you search on keywords—say, Erin's inoculation records—in what file drawer those papers are stored. It also works for locating *things*—where did I put the work boots that my son uses once a year for a church-sponsored trip? It will also locate your myriad of software disks when you are commanded to reinstall and even remind you of the contents of your safe-deposit box. It's ideal for business owners, and busy families also swear by the Paper Tiger indexing system. And for those who need help getting started, there are more than seventy authorized Paper Tiger consultants nationwide, ready to help you get up and running.

At this point, readers might ask, "To eliminate paper files, should I be scanning everything with an electronic scanner and storing all of it on my computer?" I don't recommend it. While scanning is a very helpful technology, it's also very time-consuming, and personally, I don't have the time.

In the electronic arena, desktop manageability tools and document management are categories of software that are purchased often by large corporations, but for the sake of simplicity, I believe that both the Windows and Macintosh operating systems give home and family users all the organizing tools that they need to file and locate their electronic documents. For your "soft copy" file cabinet, use the folder entitled MY DOCUMENTS on your hard drive. Create additional folders within MY DOCUMENTS as needed. If your computer has more than one user, families typically assign a folder to each family member—SUSAN'S DOCUMENTS, GEORGE'S DOCUMENTS, and so on.

To avoid one document folder with hundreds of individual documents, group pages relating to one another into their own folder. As a business owner, I of course have electronic folders for each client, as well as folders for various community involvements and groups to which I belong.

For people like Anthony L., a graphic designer who suffered from a dizzying number of icons on his computer desktop, relief can by found from a visual file cabinet on his desktop such as DragStrip (http://www.aladdinsys. com/dragstrip/winindex.html). "I no longer waste valuable time searching for electronic documents or digging through browser windows," Anthony says. Forget looking for buried Shortcuts in the Start Menu. DragStrip organizes your most frequently used files, applications, Web sites, pictures, and even sounds into one desktop launching pad. Dedicated Mac users also love FinderKeeper from Elsware Ltd. (www.elsware.com). For more solutions to desktop disarray, search on-line for the term "desktop organizers."

While we're talking about the view of your desktop, PC users of the Windows 98 operating system can add content from Web pages to their computer desktops by using

Microsoft's Active Desktop. To add this helpful organizer to your computer, right click in the desktop area and select PROPERTIES from the menu.

1. Make sure "View My Active Desktop as a Web Page" is checked.
2. Click on the NEW button.
3. A dialogue box will pop up asking if you would like to go to Microsoft's Web site to download Active Desktop components, such as stock tickers and weather forecasts.
4. Select "yes" to go to the site, or "no" if you would like to use a Web site of your choice.
5. Type in the URL of the page you would like to use.
6. If you are surfing and find a site you like, you right click on it, drag it to your desktop, and select "Create Active Desktop Items Here."

Tara M., an environmental attorney, often travels internationally, and during school vacations, she likes to bring along her teacher husband and their two kids. I was intrigued how she had customized her laptop's Active Desktop to include these helpful Web sites:

- www.fly.faa.gov for real-time flight-delay information
- www.weather.com for real-time weather information
- www.worldtimeserver.com for time anywhere in the world
- www.quickaid.com for maps of major airports

For people who use different Web browsers and want to organize all the various bookmarks that they have saved as Favorites, a bookmark utility program like Powermarks is inexpensive and helpful. You can download a free demo copy at www.kaylon.com/power.html.

How Long to Save?

The question of how long to hold on to your paper and electronic documents is always one of the first where organizing paper is concerned. Accountants and tax experts tell us that the statute of limitations on federal tax audits is three years, which means that you can actually pitch these records, and the supporting tax documents such as W-2 forms and receipts for deductions, after three years. The state where you live may have different requirements. Be sure to check.

"Investment records, such as those relating to buying a house or stocks and bonds should be kept for as long as you own them," says Scott Brenner, CPA, a partner with Dylewsky, Goldberg & Brenner in Stamford, Connecticut. "However, once you sell the asset, you should retain those records for three more years. Proof of mortgage or rental payments should also be kept for three years."

What about routine items that are not tax deductible, such as utility bills and credit card statements? You can throw these out after a year. The same is true for bank statements, canceled checks, and medical bills, as long as you're not claiming them as deductions. If you have a billing dispute, many states allow creditors to go back up to seven years. But there's no need to hang on to all those paid bills. The merchant or credit-card issuer should be able to provide it.

Weeding out unnecessary or "expired" documents from your paper file cabinets or computer hard drive should be done at least once a year, or you may find yourself just like my town hall—in search of additional, and expensive, storage space. A very helpful antidote to increasingly crowded file drawers, as well as diminishing space on your hard drive, is to give every folder an expiration date. This strategy makes purging your files much easier. If you have sold some stocks, for example, and claimed the gains or losses on your income tax returns, the folder containing those transaction records should be dated three years from that taxable year. When that year arrives, remove and toss all the papers that expire that year. There's no need to comb through the folder's contents—you already made the decision to act three years ago.

To reduce the time it takes to purge my electronic files, I date *every* document. In addition, because the vast majority of my documents are written in Microsoft Word, I make sure I have selected "Preview" when I go into File Open, which lets me glimpse the beginning of any document that I highlight in the menu list. That way, I'm viewing my documents regularly and also deleting the ones I no longer need. I'm determined to not run out of disk space before my computer has served its time!

For hard-copy papers, professional organizers recommend filing them in metal file cabinets, which are more fireproof than those made of wood or cardboard. In addition, Attorney Stuart Welkovich, of Stamford, Connecticut, encourages his clients to have a safe-deposit box in a bank, where they keep their most important papers such as deeds to property, titles to cars or other personal property, passports, birth certificates, marriage licenses, divorce decrees, a copy of their will, and so on. Also, keeping a list of what's in your safe-deposit box can save time and prevent unnecessary trips to your box when you can't remember where you've put an important paper.

"I recommend that while you may choose to keep the originals of your will and other estate planning documents in your safe-deposit box, you should retain photocopies, or scanned electronic copies, of these documents in a safe place outside of the box so your loved ones can find them when you die," says Welkovich. "The reason is that when a person dies, his safe-deposit box is often sealed by the court, or banks on their own may deny access to survivors.

"With young couples, I want to know that a copy of their will is held by a trusted friend or family member in the event, God forbid, they should *both* perish in a car accident."

There is one brief document that I keep on a floppy disk and in hard copy in the file drawer I use every day. It is unceremoniously called "Very Important Stuff," and for reasons of security (discussed later on in this chapter), I do not save a copy on my hard drive. This document lists:

- All bank, investment, and credit-card account numbers
- All passwords and PIN codes
- All utility account numbers
- The telephone numbers of my attorney and accountant
- All insurance policy numbers and telephone numbers
- A list of the contents of my safe-deposit box
- The locations of my will and other estate planning documents

On this same document, I list all my software registration numbers and key codes. Alas, I didn't start doing this until recently, and I haven't made the time to review all my software installations, but more important, I'm committed to saving this information *from now on*.

I have prepared this document, which I review every January, for the ease and comfort of my loved ones, should I become incapacitated or die. Lord knows I won't have a large estate to leave behind, but I do want to pass on the gift of good record keeping.

Backing Up

Every technology advisor I've ever spoken to stresses the inevitable: It's not a question of *if*, but rather *when* your computer will fail. How, then, do you protect your electronic documents against loss or damage? By backing them up regularly so you will always have copies if something happens to your hard drive.

In the early days of desktop computers, many people created a second backup folder on their hard drive and also backed up their most important data onto floppy disks. Today floppies are convenient for bringing a few documents to another user, who perhaps can't retrieve them from a main server or receive them by e-mail, but as backup, they are tremendously restricted by their limited storage capacity—often less than two megabytes. And who has time to back up their files onto hundreds of disks?

A Zip drive, which compresses files, became the next choice, and Zip cartridges typically hold one hundred or two hundred fifty megabytes (see www.iomega.com). However, if you store multimedia or large databases, Zip drives are soon unsuitable for full backup. The next choice for greater capacity is a CD-R (compact disk recordable) or CD-RW (compact disc rewritable) drive, which permits the user to back up data to compact discs (CDs)—up to seven hundred megabytes per disk. Next in line for increased capacity is a Jaz drive with disk, which stores up to two gigabytes.

Those who long to carry twenty gigabytes of data in their pocket should consider a miniature Pockey drive (www.pockeydrives.com). And finally, companies like On-Stream (www.onstream.com) make digital tape drives and cartridges that hold thirty gigabytes and more. These are generally considered overkill for home use, but I've seen them in several households that back up large photographic and music files.

The backup solutions that most people are accustomed to in the workplace are tape drives on network servers. Smaller companies might use a server as backup for their PCs. At home, network backup would be appropriate if you own two or more PCs or Macs and are willing to purchase and install a home network. (A home network is necessary if you have more than one computer sharing one Internet connection, and the computer running the network has to be on all the time.)

The Internet has opened up many alternatives to traditional backup. With Web backup services and virtual hard drives, you send your data to their password-protected servers, which you can then access 24/7 for a monthly fee. Two on-line backup companies reviewed very favorably by CNET.com are www.backup.net and www.connected. com. Many other options can be found by searching for "on-line backup" at any of the major search engines.

One note of caution: Charles Asmar, Internet consultant, Web site host and owner of HighestRank.com (www.highestrank.com), helped me realize that I didn't need to back up as many files as I had thought. "You need to back up data, not your entire hard drive," he cautions.

"In the event of a computer crash, programs can be reinstalled. However, your databases and documents cannot be replaced unless you have a backup."

Where PDAs are concerned, Jeff Carlson points out, "People store all sorts of sensitive materials on their handhelds and then never lock the device, hide private records, or encrypt data. To be fair, it isn't a huge issue yet, but as data becomes ever more portable and we explore all the ways in which personal data can be abused, securing that data is going to get even more important."

If you're looking for more storage space for your data, it is available for free in cyberspace from:

- Driveway (www.driveway.com)
- Xdrive (www.xdrive.com)
- FreeDrive (www.freedrive.com)
- MySpace.com (www.freediskspace.com)

After all of the controversy over MP3.com and Napster.com—the music-file-sharing Web sites—David Pakman cofounded myplay.com (www.myplay.com), which stores your music files in cyberspace. (It is also approved by the music industry because it pays royalties on music that is shared among users.) Each listener is assigned a "virtual locker," which holds at least three gigabytes' worth of files on myplay's computer servers.

These Web-based storage services permit users to access their data from any Web-connected PC. You can even create passwords that allow others to share certain files.

Remember your lifetime learning habits. Read up on these Web systems before you invest. Do they require a broadband Internet connection (cable modem or digital subscriber line) or will a 56K modem do? Do you need an automated backup routine, or are you really looking just for more storage?

Which backup system to use for *your* e-organized life is certainly a question to ask your technology advisor. The point is you want to be able to recover your essential documents in case your computer dies a sudden death, an electrical surge destroys your motherboard, or a flood or fire damages your home and computer equipment. If you don't already have a backup plan in place, protecting your data should be at the very top of your to-do list.

Security and Privacy

No discussion about protecting your electronic documents is complete without mentioning on-line security and privacy. First of all, a very simple step to take for Microsoft Windows 95 or 98 is to turn off the option that lets others look at your files:

1. Click the Windows "start" button.
2. Go to Settings and select the "Control Panel."
3. Double click the "Network" icon.
4. Click on the "File and Print-Sharing" button.
5. Uncheck the two check boxes in the new window.

Anyone who runs a business in which workers are connected to the Internet knows the importance of installing a firewall—that is, hardware or software that monitors your computer's connection to the Internet and prevents intruders from entering the network. As more people use high-speed or broadband Internet connections in their homes, and therefore leave their PCs connected to the Internet for longer periods, they are installing firewalls at home.

A popular software choice, which can be downloaded free from Zone Labs Inc. (www.zonealarm.com), is ZoneAlarm. Other software favorites are:

- Source Velocity PC Viper (www.sourcevelocity.com)
- Tiny Personal Firewall (www.tinysoftware.com)
- Norton's Personal Firewall (www.symantec.com)
- McAfee Personal Firewall (www.mcafee-at-home.com)
- Internet Guard Dog (www.mcafee-at-home.com)
- BlackICE Defender (www.networkice.com)

The Norton Internet Security Family Edition (www.symantec.com), a suite of several applications including Norton AntiVirus, is worth considering for families with multiple computers. Once you have completed the setup, you can add an account for each family member. The program allows you to customize Internet restrictions for young children and to specify the type of information that you don't want passed over the Internet, such as your credit card or telephone numbers.

Another option for families with more than one computer on-line is a *hardware* firewall such as the Linksys EtherFast 4-Port Cable/DSL Router (www.linksys.com) for Windows or Mac. Devotees of this router tell me it's also a great product for simple networking and for replacing your DSL (digital subscriber line) modem. Furthermore, there is a one-port version of this product. "The benefit of a hardware solution is there is no overhead on the PC since it is always on and doesn't need to restart each time the PC starts," says Allen O'Farrell. "Also, it logically separates the PC from the Internet, rather than filters stuff."

Whether or not you have a broadband Internet connection, if you connect to the Internet at all, download files, or exchange e-mail, computer viruses pose a serious threat. The antidote is a sturdy antivirus program, such as:

- Panda Antivirus (www.pandasoftware.com)
- McAfee VirusScan (www.mcafee.com)
- Norton AntiVirus (www.symantec.com)

Unfortunately, with the increase in the number of computer viruses has come an increase in virus *hoaxes*. To keep from being made the fool, I always check the Norton AntiVirus Web site every time I receive an e-mail virus warning. Go to http://www.symantec.com; then put the virus name in the search box.

Assuming that *your* computers are protected against viruses and hacking intruders, what about the other guys? How do you make security and privacy a part of your on-line shopping, on-line banking, on-line investing, and so on?

Joanne Kabak, a journalist who covers Internet issues, defines a *secure* on-line transaction as one in which your data has been encoded so that no one except the intended receiver can decipher it. A *private* transaction, on the other hand, means that the recipient is not selling your data to another company.

There are a number of steps that consumers can take to shop safely on the Web, according to Vickery Kehlenbeck, a Boston-based attorney with the law firm of Robinson & Cole LLP (www.rc.com):

- Look for and read a site's privacy policy. It should state what information they are gathering and what they're going to do with it.

- Look for sites that display seals from the Better Business Bureau (BBBOnLine) or TRUSTe. These retailers have agreed to an outside review of their policies.
- Determine that the site is secure by finding a closed padlock or key symbol in the lower corner of your browser.
- At the point where you submit credit card or other personal information, examine the URL (uniform resource locator) or address. If it begins with *https://*, instead of the usual *http://*, that means your data will be secure.

"Use common sense," Kabak adds. "Legitimate e-tailers need your name, address, phone, and e-mail to complete an on-line transaction, but they don't need your Social Security number or bank account number."

Many people prefer the convenience of on-line banking. Most banks with an Internet presence allow their customers to pay bills and transfer money from one account to another. Technically speaking, they require that your Web browser support 128-bit encryption. This means that your information is scrambled before it leaves your computer, thereby protecting your financial information from being viewed by hackers.

The U.S. Congress has encouraged these kinds of activities by passing the Electronic Signature law in the summer of 2000. Now you can open a mutual fund account on-line—your "signature" is the password you assign to the account. With Fidelity Investments, for example, your signature is your Social Security number, plus a PIN that you select. It is possible to make investments with Fidelity by transferring funds from your bank account, rather than sending a check, and when you wish to make a withdrawal, your account can be set up so that your proceeds go into the cash or other account that you specify. No paper—all electronic.

For those who are squeamish about the absence of a paper trail where their money is concerned, rest assured that you can't be forced to use an e-signature. A company has to provide a paper contract if you ask for one.

I shop on-line often. To remember the details of my purchases, I always save an electronic copy of my purchase order in a folder for ALL ORDERS. If you are a frequent on-line shopper like me, you may find it difficult to remember all your user names and passwords. Gator.com (www.gator.com) offers a secure and sensible solution. It's a free Web browser companion that keeps track of your log-in information for all your favorite e-tailers. First you visit the site and download the free software. You will be asked to provide your name, mailing address, phone, and e-mail, along with credit card information. When you next make an on-line purchase, enter your Gator user name and password. Gator then captures and stores your log-in information for that site. The next time you return, Gator will log you on. Karen R., a confessed e-shopoholic, says, "It's so much easier to remember *one* password instead of keeping track of dozens."

One final note on the issue of security: Users continue to argue whether computers should be left on or turned off when not in use. Proponents of the former view hold that continually turning your computer on and off increases problems and decreases the computer's lifespan. However, there's another indisputable fact: When your computer is off, *it is secure.*

A Regular Appointment

My experiences as an organizing coach tell me that people seldom need guidance on what files to keep as much as they need solutions to bulging file folders and overflowing file cabinets. Rather than suggestions on where to put paper, people long for strategies for weeding out the deadwood. It's all about making the time to do it, which is the second requirement for a paper processing system: a regular appointment for your paper tasks.

Sarah W., introduced earlier in the chapter, says she accomplishes most of her paper tasks in brief moments found between more important activities. As a matter of fact, she reserves one section of her briefcase for holding quick paper tasks. However, "for the 'biggies,' like getting my income tax papers ready for my accountant or filling out my kids' applications for summer camp, I identify a block of time and note the tasks in my PDA calendar," she says.

Jonathan P., a college professor, has found his own solution. "I used to disappear into my home office every night and spend hours doing paperwork," he recalls. Then one of Jonathan's two children became seriously ill and was hospitalized. The child has fully recovered now, but the life-threatening illness caused Jonathan to reorder his priorities. He now reserves most evenings and weekends for his family. "Now I go to my campus office one hour earlier each day during the week, and I delegate more of my paperwork to my research assistant, who's only too happy to earn extra money."

Sarah and Jonathan have found different ways of managing their paper, but both are staying on top of it by committing to a routine with regular appointments. They are also practitioners of a tickler file—the third and final piece of a paper-management system.

A Tickler File for Pending Papers

Sarah's kids bring home from school a lot of paper, much of which requires that dates be entered in the family's computer calendar (synced with Sarah's PDA), or call for a parent's signature and possibly an accompanying check. Sarah has taught her children that everything goes in her in box in the family room. After supper, Sarah puts many of those papers in her "tickler file"—the folders that store the documents that she wants to resurface on a certain date.

Most hard-copy tickler files consist of thirty-one folders, labeled 1 through 31 for each day of the month, and twelve more labeled for each month of the year. Here is where you file papers that relate to your meeting on the tenth (in folder 10), catalogues you want to share with your contractor when he comes on the twenty-fourth (in folder 24), your parents' anniversary card that you want to mail on the thirtieth (in folder 30), and so on for the current month. Papers corresponding to dates in the future go in the appropriate month's folder.

Your tickler file is a solution to piles of "pending" papers that are waiting to be used on a certain date. Reduce your clutter and put them in your tickler file. It's also an answer for Mike, beleaguered business owner and father of four who laments that he "can't find anything." Rather than tearing your hair out while you search madly for misplaced papers that you need *right now*, subscribe to the organization of a tickler file and *know* where they are—in their due date's folder.

On the first day of each month, tickler users typically remove what's in that month's folder and distribute the papers into the appropriate numbered days of that month. This is quickly accomplished by Sarah, who routinely highlights the due date on each piece of paper. Some users also choose to eliminate folders for the dates corresponding to weekend days in the month—and you would certainly do this for your tickler file at work—tucking them temporarily at the back of the numbered files. The same would apply to dates when you will be out of town—on business or on vacation. Finally, I recommend that users pull up the next day's folder during the afternoon or evening before so you can see what actions are coming up. This is especially helpful for parents who are sending their children's papers back to school very early the next morning.

Mike is ecstatic with his tickler file. "Finally, I have the papers I need on the day that I need them!" Working with a professional organizer, it took Mike several evenings to reduce the clutter that had built up, but he's a zealous convert to a tickler system and is enjoying the extra time saved by not having to look for lost papers.

Let's recap the steps for implementing a tickler file:

1. Purchase forty-three file folders that are preprinted or that you label with the numbers 1 through 31 and with the twelve months of the year. Place these in your most convenient file drawer.
2. As you receive documents, place in these folders all papers that you will need to use on a certain due date. Papers for the eighth go in the 8 folder, and so on. Papers requiring your attention beyond the current month should be filed in the appropriate future month's folder.
3. Every evening take out the folder for the next day to see what's in store.

4. Each day act on those papers.
5. On the first day of a new month, distribute that month's papers into the appropriate folders.
6. Optional: At the beginning of a new month, remove folders for dates on which you don't want to do paperwork, such as weekends or vacations.

Keeping Track of People

Can you remember when you kept the names, addresses, and phone numbers of your friends, family, and business associates in an address book? They were limited in capacity and time-consuming when you ran out of pages and had to copy the contents into a new book. Paper Rolodexes were an improvement in that you could add and update the information by merely adding or changing a card, but they lacked an important feature for an e-organized life: portability. When you wanted to hand over the name of a friend to another friend, you might have said, "All my addresses and phone numbers are at home. I'll give you a call with that information."

Since the arrival of computers, we've been able to maintain and update our "address books" electronically, thanks to user-friendly databases and other software programs. And now with portable PDAs, we can bring our contacts with us wherever we go. Late for an appointment? You have the number to call with you. When you want to pass a referral to a colleague, you have the information at your fingertips on your PDA. Furthermore, sharing this information is a snap with the infrared transfer of data.

PDAs today, just like computers, come with an electronic address book built into the applications suite. Using your PDA's software on your desktop or laptop computer, you simply enter your contacts into that program. However, if you've been using e-mail or PIM (personal information manager) software at work, chances are you've already accumulated a stash of e-mail addresses and other contact information. In this case, you also have the option of "importing" your preferred database or CRM program into your PDA. For example, I chose to import my ACT! (www.act.com) database. Transitioning to an electronic system takes time and commitment. Strategies for getting the job done are discussed in chapter 5.

Just as I mentioned in chapter 1, if all you need is a Web-based electronic Rolodex, you don't need to buy a special application. Data-sharing address books are available for free from sites such as Freshaddress.com (www.freshaddress.com) and JungleMate.com (www.JungleMate.com). However, if you intend to log on to your account from your Web-enabled PDA, make sure that your service is reliable and that your contacts are easy to access.

If in the course of your life you receive a lot of paper business cards, a card scanner is a time-saving device that takes in the data much faster than you can type it. Machines such as CardScan (www.cardscan.com) do not remove the need for an editor's eye (most reviewers give it a 97 percent accuracy rate), but they are fast, and more important, the technology organizes the data and places it into the correct fields. And CardScan interacts easily with the major contact manager programs as well as handheld devices.

If you're not up to the hefty cost ($250-plus) of the CardScan Executive, you can use your existing flatbed scanner and just buy the CardScan software. This way you scan multiple cards simultaneously via the plastic cardholder, which is included.

Need to capture people's e-mail addresses from the many e-mails you receive? Adding these contacts can be as quick as a mouse click, thanks to AddressGrabber Deluxe, which transfers names and addresses from the Web, e-mail, and text documents into your address book. Sign up for a free trial from eGrabber.com (www.egrabber.com).

Last, if you desire to carry your contacts in your mobile phone, you'll want to save time by purchasing Open-Wave's FoneSync PRO (www.openwave.com), which synchronizes your whole world of contact names, phone numbers, and calendars stored on your PC with the memory in your wireless phone. It is compatible with 350 phones and the most popular PIM (personal information management) software products, including ACT! 2000, Goldmine 5.0, Lotus Notes5, Lotus Organizer6 and Microsoft Outlook 2000. Any changes made in your digital phone or on your PC or PDA are updated automatically.

An Electronic Tickler File

Rick A., a management consultant who's very enthusiastic about his paper tickler file, asked, "Is there an *electronic* version of a tickler file?" Yes, Rick, there is.

As I mentioned above, I use the CRM software ACT! (www.act.com) and have used similar programs when I worked in corporations. These powerful applications integrate your address book with your calendar and to-do list and behave like a tickler file. The primary difference is that all your data is stored alphabetically under each addressee, or contact, rather than with a specific date.

When you are in your CRM program and you create an e-mail for one of your contacts, for example, that e-mail becomes a part of that contact's history. If you need to follow up, one mouse click takes you to your calendar where you enter the necessary task.

According to Jan Wallen, an expert in CRM software, "Users learn what they have to do each day by looking at that date's electronic schedule, but you find your tickler folder contents under the appropriate contact's 'history.' For example, if you read that you have to call John at eleven a.m., a quick click to John's contact record tells you, under Notes/History, what the call's about and what's happened before and it contains copies of all relevant documents. In fact, before telephoning, e-mailing, or meeting with anyone, you can review all of the activity and the electronic documents. This is the equivalent of bringing your paper tickler folder to the meeting."

"CRM saved my life," says Sharon Z., a wedding planner. "Details don't fall through the cracks anymore. Now I keep every bride's information, and all my correspondence with her, in one place—electronically under her name—so I can find it immediately."

For your family life, CRMs can be used to provide reminders of birthdays, anniversaries, and other celebrations, to create holiday newsletters to friends far and wide, and to note important facts. For example, I know a grandmother who has created custom fields to keep track of the sizes for twenty-four members of her family.

"If you volunteer for your PTA or coach a youth baseball team and you have to remember to complete a series of tasks before each meeting or practice, your CRM calendar can be set up to remind you, *and your group of fellow volunteers,* automatically of what needs to be done," Jan explains.

Just like anything new, CRMs require commitment and practice, but once you're set up, all the extra free time you're going to enjoy is your enviable reward.

If you feel your needs do not warrant a sophisticated CRM program, you can create the semblance of a tickler system in your electronic calendar. When you note, for example, that you want to call Helen one week from today, you will save time if you include Helen's phone number with the entry and the locations of any relevant documents. This way you'll be reminded to call on the appropriate date, and you'll be directed to documents that will help you review what's happened before.

Coping with Paper Backlog

I have offered paper-managing suggestions to many clients. Most absorb the techniques outlined above the way a sponge absorbs water. However, Roger J., an advertising copywriter and new father of twins, articulates a common frustration: "If I practice your solutions faithfully *from now on*, I'm still left with the huge mess I created before I learned the Hedrick Method. What do I do with all the piles, all the files, all the *stuff* that I had accumulated before I met you?"

I return to two key points I made earlier in the chapter: (1) clutter is postponed decision making, and (2) it's all about making the time to do it, which, you will recall, is the second requirement for a paper processing system—a regular appointment for your paper tasks. I deal exhaustively with personal accountability in chapter 5, but briefly, if you want to eliminate piles, schedule the time for these tasks, one at a time, in your electronic calendar.

As for the decision-making part, as everyone knows, life is seldom black or white. Many of our decisions—including what to save and what to toss—fall into the gray area. A solution I've been using for many years is what I call "a halfway house"—that is, halfway to the garbage can or recycling bin. This is an effective and reassuring answer for people who are fearful of making a wrong decision.

Why do people fear throwing something away? Because they're afraid they'll get rid of something they're going to need after all. To prevent such a mistake, I routinely fill cartons with papers, clothing, and all manner of no-longer-needed goods. I label those cartons with a date two years in the future and tuck them away in a corner of a dry storage area—garage, basement, attic—whatever. On the appointed date, into the garbage they go!

Processing Piles of Reading

Another complaint I hear often is, "I have so much to read! I'll never get to the bottom of the pile." Let's look at three individuals who have developed their own timesaving methods for getting out from under what can be an overwhelming pile of paper:

*My friend **Julie J.**, a business consultant, subscribes to twenty-two different business magazines. She skims the tables of contents of her business magazines and tears out the most important articles, which she carries with her and reads during waiting time or in other spare moments.*

***Warren L.**, an accountant, receives reams of information from the federal and state governments concerning* *tax laws and compliance. Rather than reading every word, he reads groups of words and ideas. This is what Abby Marks-Beale, owner of The Reading Edge (www.the-reading-edge.com), calls "phrasing." She teaches her audiences how to "preview" an article, that is, how to read the first paragraph, the first sentence of every paragraph, and then the closing paragraph. Warren has also learned to find the "summaries" or "conclusions" of accounting articles, which he says contain the essentials of what he needs to know.*

*And **Melinda P.**, as a children's librarian, must constantly read review copies of new children's books and additional reviews in the trade press of those books she doesn't receive. She reads only one quarter of her reading pile, delegating the other three quarters to her fellow librarians. They convene once a week to share their insights and opinions. I've observed research chemists use this "reading team" technique, as well as the IT divisions in large corporations. "There's so much to keep current on," Melinda says. "No one person can do it all, so we divide and conquer."*

If, after trying the coping strategies above, your reading mountain is still too tall, Abby recommends "putting your pile on a diet":

- Heave whatever remains unread longer than two weeks into your recycling bin.
- "Unsubscribe" to all but the essential papers, newsletters, and magazines. If you learn of a must-read cover story, buy it at the newsstand.
- Always carry reading materials with you, tossing them when read.

- Retain only the pieces that require specific actions. Enter the actions in your electronic calendar and file the papers in your tickler file.

All the above mentioned coping strategies apply to on-line subscriptions as well as to paper.

One final point about staying abreast of your reading: "Even though I always coach people to reduce their reading pile in snatches of time, reading requires concentration," according to Abby. "We all know the sensation of reading a paragraph, then reading it again and sometimes again, but not absorbing it. Either there are too many other distractions or you're too tired. Reading to understand requires quiet surroundings and your peak energy."

Reading On-line

The same can be said for doing research on-line: It requires your full attention and takes a lot of time. Are there techniques and strategies to help you be more productive? Yes, and not surprisingly, the best tips and shortcuts can be found in the Help screens of search *directories*, such as Yahoo (www.yahoo.com), Go (www.go.com), or Excite (www.excite.com), or of search *engines*, such as Altavista (www.altavista.com) or Hotbot (http://hotbot.lycos.com/).

Practicing research on the Internet will hone your skills and reduce your search time. Brad Fisher, entrepreneur and e-commerce guru, says, "People who commit to visiting at least one new Web site every day get better at it—they find what they're looking for more quickly and eventually develop Web intuition."

However, according to Lisa Guernsey, a technology reporter at the *New York Times*, traditional search engines have access to only a fraction of 1 percent of what really exists on the Web. Expert searchers know how to mine the "invisible Web" by using specialized directories, such as Completeplanet (www.completeplanet.com). An overview of these search engines can be found at Search Engine Watch (www.searchenginewatch.com). Another useful tool, launched in April 2001, is iLOR (www.ilor.com), which tries to improve the process of shuffling through search results by eliminating much of the tedious navigation.

A fine example of an individual who has progressed from Internet novice to "surfing" pro is Tom A., who retired from his career in marketing last summer and set about taking charge of his finances on-line. When I told him all that I was learning about the invisible Web, Tom said he had just located the specialized directory at FinancialFind.com (www.financialfind.com), which helped him locate financial planning and investment sites, including those that offer tax information.

Tom discovered two sites that give him specific advice on how to invest his 401(k)—Financial Engines (www.financialengines.com) and ClearFuture (www.morningstar.com). For looking at his portfolio by sector and market capitalization, Tom uses the free services at SmartMoney.com (www.smartmoney.com). To improve his trading-related decision-making and chart-reading skills, he swears by the helpful resources at Tradetrek.com (www.tradetrek.com). And finally, he regularly checks the best rates for money-market accounts and CDs (certificates of deposit) at Money Rates (www.money-rates.com).

Tom's goal—to dive into the Internet, mine what it offers for his financial planning needs, and to do so *productively*— is an excellent example of improving e-literacy by practicing lifetime learning habits, which leads us quite naturally to the next chapter on setting goals.

Chapter 3

You Have Written Goals and Specific Timetables for Accomplishing Them

*A*llison F. *has just been pink slipped. She was termi-
nated from her job two weeks ago and can't focus on
looking for work. On the one hand, she suspects that being let go may be a blessing in disguise because she really
didn't enjoy her job that much anyway. But like everyone
else, Allison has expenses and bills to pay and must find
employment. Should she change fields? Should she relo-
cate? She has many questions about what to do next.*

*Jack M. is a successful thirty-six-year-old business
owner who would like to get married. All of the women
he meets through his job seem to be married or spoken
for. He feels at a loss to spark up his social life, to enliven
those lonely weekends and thus increase his chances of
finding Miss Right.*

*Nadine W. says she wants to nurture her emotional
and spiritual self. She has moved away from a busy urban
center and cut back her full-time work to three days a
week. But her plan to slow down keeps getting sabotaged.
Nadine is highly skilled and much in demand; employers
for her freelance promotion work keep calling. So far she's
been able to say no to the extra work, but she doesn't
know where to turn to find the emotional and spiritual*

support she's searching for. She's afraid that, once again, she will simply fill the void with more work.

What happened in each of the three examples above? In each case, the individual has a vague idea of what he or she is looking for or wants to accomplish, but no one has looked at that wish or situation as a concrete problem to be solved. The "problems" are clear enough, but the solutions are kind of swimming around in their heads—amorphous, undefined.

"Goals—or problems needing solutions—mean nothing unless they're written," insists Midé Wilkey, executive coach and portfolio manager for Montauk Financial Group, Stamford, Connecticut. In this chapter, you will learn to use one of the most important timesaving techniques at your disposal—goal setting. Now it's time to learn the steps for writing long-term goals for all the areas of your life—your family, your home, your health, your community, your faith—and for developing the strategies for accomplishing them. Men and women who learn and practice these techniques are more productive and lead richer, fuller lives.

Goal-Setting Requirements

The first step to committing your goals to writing requires two things: a quiet place and some quiet time. I realize that carving out some personal time far away from distractions is a major accomplishment for many extremely busy people. However, if you can create the right environment, you will save a lot of time in your goal-setting exercise. If your attention is diverted by squabbling children, loud music, or other distractions, it's likely that what is a very fun and creative opportunity will become frustrating drudgery. In addition, your search for problem solutions will be aided by your brain if it is focused on what is really important to you.

What tools do you need? In addition to some quiet time in a quiet place, all you need is your computer or PDA or, if you prefer, a scratch pad and pencil.

The first step in goal setting is to write the goal so that it is *realistic, specific,* and *measurable*. Doing so will save you time, but more important, realistic, specific, and measurable goals are much more likely to be accomplished. For example, which goals stand the best chance of successful completion?

(a) Lose weight.
(b) Lose ten pounds in the next six months by eliminating desserts and by walking two miles at least four times a week.

(a) Increase "quality time" for the family.
(b) Plan one two-hour outing each weekend that we all do together.

(a) Earn more money.
(b) Within thirty days write a one-page case for why I deserve a salary raise, and make an appointment with my boss to discuss it.

(a) Get more energy.
(b) Within a week, make an appointment for a medical checkup to discuss my chronic fatigue.

Obviously, the *b*s are favored to succeed, even though each *b* is only one of many possible strategies for achieving *a*. The *b* choices are more user-friendly; they invite the goal setter in. Even if the *b* goal is too intimidating—I could *never* give up all desserts for six months!—you can keep reworking the words until they ring true *for you.*

Let's revisit the three individuals at the beginning of this chapter. Allison needs to get a job; no doubt about that. But I suspect that her initial goal is more precisely to study her employment options. It's hard enough being laid off or fired, but to her credit, Allison has pinpointed the fact that she wasn't very happy or satisfied in her last job, and she's determined that her next situation will not duplicate that dissatisfaction. Allison resolves to spend one month assessing her skills and talents and targeting appropriate employers and job descriptions.

Jack, the lonely bachelor, longs to be married, but he's smart enough to know that a more *realistic, specific, and measurable* goal would be to improve his social life. "Going from zero to one would be a start," he says with a laugh. After struggling for a few minutes, Jack writes, "Put myself in situations where I can meet single women my age." Honing his goal even further, he comes up with: "Once a week and once every weekend I will explore 'meeting' opportunities on-line, as well as go to places and events where I will meet single women my own age." Well-done goal setting!

And Nadine, our final example, wants to nourish her soul, and that's a very legitimate goal. She doesn't know where she will find her nourishment or what forms it will take, but nevertheless, she knows she must quantify this important objective. Nadine writes, "I will devote at least one day every week to researching on-line, and in person at various community centers, what my geographic area offers in the way of support groups and classes in matters spiritual, and I will 'try on' at least one opportunity each week." Bravo, Nadine!

Goals for Every Area of Your Life

What about you? What are your goals? What problems would you like to solve in any area of your life? Midé Wilkey identifies six categories for every individual's goals:

1. Home and family—our most intimate connections
2. Social—our friendships and community life
3. Physical—our health, fitness, nutrition, and so forth
4. Mental—using our minds
5. Spiritual life—from what we derive meaning
6. Career and financial—most often the easiest to address

You can choose to write goals for all six categories, or to begin with one or two—wherever you're comfortable. The first step is to articulate your wishes in writing and to keep them close at hand—their own icon on your computer's desktop, in the Memo Pad on your PDA, or in hard copy—whichever works best for you.

"Goals are intended to be read and reviewed regularly so you can sustain your focus on them," Wilkey adds.

The Next Step: Brainstorming

The second step in problem solving, or goal setting, is to brainstorm. Used by people in all areas of life, to brainstorm means, literally, to "storm the brain," to produce a flood of ideas. Companies come up with inspirations for new products and names for those products by brainstorming, schools generate new areas of their curricula, and concerned groups of citizens create solutions to community problems through this intuitive process. Many of us have participated in such a brainstorming session in which a group sets out to solve a problem through the spontaneous contribution of ideas from all members. It's an effective technique, and you as an individual can use it just as successfully.

In its simplest form, bite-size brainstorming means making a list. The list you make may not be complete, but that doesn't matter. What matters is that you've started—and you're moving.

When you begin to brainstorm as a committee of one, you open your mental floodgates and let all your ideas and thoughts about how to accomplish your goal flow freely. Write anything and everything that comes to mind; write continuously, and don't stop to edit. There are no right or wrong answers. Everything is acceptable, and the order of the tasks listed is not important. What you are trying to do is list *all* the bites.

You're looking for a spontaneous flow of ideas, but more specifically, you're looking for the smaller parts of the whole. That's why I call it bite-size brainstorming. The object of brainstorming when you're trying to get e-organized is more than just free-associating—the purpose is to break down a goal into its smallest parts. Organizing consultants compare this strategy to eating an elephant—one bite at a time. The goal that seems unattainable when looked at as a whole (so much so that you're likely to abandon it altogether) becomes manageable when broken into its bite-size components. It's just human nature to be more accepting of smaller tasks than of larger projects. Failing to perform this important step may be one of the reasons why you've failed to complete goals in the past.

Here's the trick: Brainstorm each step of your elephant-size goal down into smaller and smaller substeps until you finally say, "That's it. I've got it. I can do that. I want to do that. I'm going to do that." If you haven't achieved those feelings, you haven't broken down far enough. Go back and break down some more.

How long will your list be? That depends on the size of your elephant. How long does bite-size brainstorming take? Usually a few minutes, but again, that depends on the girth of your pachyderm.

Let's look at some goals, and their bite-size lists, that relate to getting e-organized. I know easily three dozen friends and acquaintances who say they long to abandon their paper Rolodexes and join the digital age. In most cases these people are small business owners who are extremely busy. They *know* they waste time by not using PIM (personal information management) or CRM (customer relationship management) software, but throw up their hands in despair at the magnitude and complexity of their problem. Solution? Let's start with some bites listed by Steven R.:

- Search the Internet for information on "electronic address books."
- Check the library and local bookstore for information and product reviews.
- Look at and ask advice about electronic address books at office supply or computer stores.
- Visit homes and offices of my friends who use electronic address books and related software.
- Ask fellow business owners how they coped with the

transition process, learning curve, data entry tasks, and the like.

Do these bites have a familiar ring to them? To me, they bear a strong resemblance to the *lifetime learning habits* introduced in chapter 1:

- Read, on-line and off-.
- View and try demos.
- Shop, but don't buy . . . yet.
- Ask, ask, ask.
- Share tips with colleagues.

Steven has the right idea: Before he can begin to make the actual transition, he has to *research* his options. "It's still off-putting," he complains. "I don't have time to go to libraries and bookstores and computer stores." Solution? Make the bites smaller.

- Send an e-mail to six friends asking them what electronic address book they use and why.
- Visit one office supply store this Saturday.
- Visit my friend Mark's office at the end of the day to observe his PIM software.
- Call Sally. She reads computer magazines. Which one would she recommend for my problem?
- Using one Internet search engine, print out the results of one search, and read it over the weekend.
- Call John. Maybe his son, the "geek," has some suggestions.

This time Steven is right on the mark. Each bite of his elephant—and he still has many more ideas to add to his list—is one single task.

"Now I get it," he remarks. "I was repulsed by the

thought of spending hours at a bookstore or searching on-line, but I *can* make a phone call, send an e-mail, or visit one store."

Suzanne A. lives in the United States but has an import business with, as well as family in, the Philippines. Her casual reading about world telecommunications convinced her to give serious consideration to Internet telephony—that is, making international phone calls and sending faxes over the Internet, which is much cheaper than traditional calling and faxing. So installing Internet telephony—so-called voice-over IP (Internet protocol)—is Suzanne's elephant. Here is her bite-size brainstorm:

- Check out *Telephony* magazine, www.internettelephony.com
- Talk to my T-coach.
- Which calls and faxes should go over IP, and which should be handled the traditional way?
- Gather three years of phone bills to look at calling patterns.
- Do I want to use the public Internet, or a voice-over-IP provider that operates its own IP network?
- Understand the difference between PC-to-phone calling and phone-to-phone calling.
- Try out Internet telephony at Charles's office.
- Estimate how often I will call and fax the Philippines.
- Check out another magazine, *Internet Telephony*, www.tmcnet.com
- What additional hardware, if any, do I need to buy?
- Try out Internet telephony at Diana's home.
- Research online voice-over-IP providers, including: CallServe (www.callserve.com)

     Dialpad Communications (www.dialpad.com)
     IconnectHere (www.iconnecthere.com)
     MediaRing.com (www.mediaring.com)
     Net2Phone.com (www.net2phone.com)
     NetVoice (www.netvoice.com)

Suzanne has made a very good beginning. Notice her tasks are listed in random order, just as she thought of them. She will no doubt add more bites to her list, but she did an excellent job of breaking down the project into individual tasks.

Long-Term Goals

Jane Pollak, an artist, entrepreneur, and motivational speaker who leads workshops on goal setting (www.jane-pollak.com), makes an important distinction between a short-term and long-term goal. For Jane, a short-term goal is something that she can accomplish in two to three weeks. A long-term goal, on the other hand, is most often a project with a lot of pieces. "Call it several goals within one large goal," she explains.

A common long-term goal frequently addressed in one of Jane's goal-setting workshops is to establish a Web site. Entrepreneurs, small-business owners, and even hobbyists are recognizing the enormous potential of the World Wide Web. But this is a huge undertaking, a large elephant with many subelephants, if you will.

For getting one's arms around a large project like building a Web site, Jane recommends the technique known as *mind mapping.* Coined by Tony Buzan in the 1970s, mind mapping means drawing a picture of a project rather than starting at the top of a page and working down in phrases, as you would if you wrote a traditional outline. Instead, you start by writing your goal, or project, inside a circle at the center of your page, and then you draw "legs" out from the circle to represent smaller parts of the whole.

"On a piece of scratch paper you make a circle in the center of the page and label that circle 'establish a Web site,' " Jane explains. "Then you draw lines out from the center circle, like a spider's legs, and those legs have little bodies with more legs.

"The idea—just as with bite-size brainstorming—is to write down everything you think of around the central goal, but most important, the order doesn't matter."

On the next page is an illustration of a mind map for setting up a Web site.

As you can see, the illustration is really an elaborate bite-size brainstorm. Obviously, there are many parts to developing a presence on the Internet, and for each of those parts you would generate a list of the bites.

Can you do mind mapping on your computer? Absolutely, thanks to the software developed by the Bosley Group (www.mindmapper.com). MindMapper is an inexpensive, graphics-based method of taking notes, brainstorming, and organizing thoughts that helps you relate and arrange random ideas into treelike diagrams.

Looking for a new job, as Allison F. must do, is another example of a long-term goal that consists of several parts. After Allison completes her first short-term goal of assessing her skills and talents and identifying appropriate job categories, she will have to pull together a new resume, outline her search strategy, perhaps hone her interviewing skills, and so on. In the process of assessment, she may decide to acquire some additional skills. Since Allison is a devoted user of her PDA, she writes and stores her

Words & photos
Links to e-mail
Merchant account for credit card processing

Do I want a Web bulletin board?
Check message-board software and user reviews

Outline possible page content
Key messages for the viewer
Products and services
Target market
Purpose

Hire Web development co.: www.bcentral.com
Buy software—do it myself
Hire student of HTML

Outline Content for Web Site

Figure Out Method to Develop Site

Establish My Web Site

Research Ways to Drive Traffic to Site

www.highestrank.com

Register a Domain Name

Find a Web-Hosting Service

Visit a Web-hosting search engine:
www.ispcheck.com

www.networksolutions.com
www.register.com
www.namesecure.com
Full directory of registration services:
www.internic.net

Example of a Mind Map

brainstorming lists in her Memo Pad. They might look like this:

✎ *Research my options*
- List my skills and talents.
- List my work dreams and fantasies.
- E-mail, call, and meet with friends for ideas and referrals.
- Contact continuing education centers concerning their course offerings.
- Join on-line forums concerning job transitions.
- Find a job transition support group.
- Read a book on job change.

✎ *Update my resume*
- Hire a coach.
- Take a course.
- Join a support group.
- Read a book.
- Draft my revisions and get feedback.
- Research on line resume help, such as www.jobwhiz.net.

✎ *My marketing strategy*
- Read job listings, on-line and off-.
- Apply to appropriate job openings.
- Network with my network.
- Target companies recognized for employee development.
- Search their Web sites for job openings.

It should be possible to list the bites for any goal, personal or professional. And certainly different people will list different tasks even if their goals are identical. But it's crucial that you get down to the smallest possible bite. It's also important to point out that a bite-size brainstorm, or mind map, is a work in progress. Once you start turning the gear works of your mind, you will continue to think of more bites. You will throw out some that you wrote before and add new ones. Nothing is carved in stone.

Are you concerned that by having so many lists you will become buried in minutia? In fact, when you brainstorm to break up something large into smaller pieces you really *are* looking at the big picture. Bite-size brainstorming as a step in the e-organizing process is often skipped because people haven't understood the importance of looking at the whole elephant. In their haste to get the most accomplished, they plunged into a pile of tasks without having any idea how many parts there are between the elephant's tusks and its tail. The result? They never finish the elephant.

If you bite-size brainstorm first, you give yourself the opportunity to think of every possible contingency, every detail. You may not need to do every bite that you've listed, but by beginning a project in this manner, you won't miss anything or forget something en route to getting it done, and you will be better prepared for the unpredictable bites ahead. In other words, *brainstorming saves time*.

"I felt overwhelmed by the thought of looking for a new job," Allison admits. "But bite-size brainstorming is fun and energizing. I feel terrific!"

Her reaction is typical. Getting started makes you feel good about yourself. Your lists may not be complete, but that doesn't matter. What matters is that you've started—and you're moving. This boosts your morale and provides an added bonus: a burst of energy that you can apply to doing the tasks you've listed.

Thoughts Versus Actions

Further refinement of bite-size brainstorming is to identify the *action* bites of an elephant. In writing lists for the "get a new job" goal, people new to the brainstorming process frequently offer decision or thinking bites rather than action bites. For example, they might say, "First I must think about what I don't like about my old job. Then I must think about what I like to do. Then I must think about what I'm good at, what my skills are."

All of these are valid; these decisions have to be made. But at this rate, Allison will never get out of her thinking posture and on with her life. Anyone looking for a job, or wanting to change jobs, already has a lot of information about what she doesn't like to do and what she does, and it's only by identifying and performing *actions* that she will achieve her goal and make a change.

Look at the examples below where I've listed different goals, each followed by a thinking bite and an action bite:

1. **Goal:** *Get a new job.*
   Think about: *What I like to do.*
   Action: *Research employment Web sites like Monster.com and HotJobs.com*
2. **Goal:** *Add music to my Web site.*
   Think about: *What styles and selections are appropriate.*
   Action: *Hire my tech advisor to do it.*
3. **Goal:** *Learn HTML (Hypertext Markup Language), the Internet programming language.*
   Think about: *Various education centers that might offer it.*
   Action: *Enroll at an on-line learning Web site.*
4. **Goal:** *Convert to an electronic address book or*

CRM (customer relationship management) program.

Think about: *The software features I will need.*

Action: *Enter the data for five contacts every morning before I start my job.*

5. **Goal:** *Organize all my software disks, papers, manuals, and so on.*

    Think about: *Where to store it.*

    Action: *Purchase disk storage, file folders, and other organizers, at the office supply store.*

6. **Goal:** *Take a vacation in France.*

    Think about: *Where in France I might like to go—Provence or Dordogne.*

    Action: *Get information from the French tourist office and join an on-line chat forum for people in search of off-season bargains in France.*

7. **Goal:** *Write a book.*

    Think about: *When I will schedule blocks of writing time.*

    Action: *Order Elizabeth Lyons's* Nonfiction Book Proposals Anyone Can Write *(http://www. elizabethlyon.com/books.htm).*

8. **Goal:** *Reduce my to-read pile.*

    Think about: *What publications are necessary for me to stay current in my field.*

    Action: *Cancel six hard-copy magazine subscriptions in favor of on-line summaries.*

9. **Goal:** *Infuse my "in-a-rut" social life with new people and new activities.*

    Think about: *What I would enjoy doing for fun.*

    Action: *Pick up a program brochure at the local arts center.*

10. **Goal:** *Switch to a broadband Internet connection.*

Think about: *The need to add firewall protection.*
Action: *E-mail four friends to learn whether they prefer a cable modem or a DSL (digital subscriber line) service and why.*

It is not my intention to diminish the importance of creative thinking tasks. From composing a jingle to plotting a prosecution, from writing a slogan to outlining a program of medical treatment, from designing a logo to planning a family's menu, thought is the germ of creation. It's just that you must not stop with thinking but must carry the thought through by doing.

When you look at several brainstorming lists side by side, you'll notice that certain tasks appear regularly, such as "do on-line research," "ask my friends what they use," and "download the software to take advantage of thirty-day free trial." Translated, these bites represent the some of the *lifetime learning habits* that are the cornerstones of problem solving. You'll find similar bites on many of your brainstorming lists.

This is a technique to help you get started, a way to orient yourself mentally. If you start to bite-size brainstorm but the blank screen keeps staring back at you, you can ask yourself.

- What should I read, on-line and off-?
- What demos can I view and try?
- Where should I window-shop?
- Which friends should I ask?

How to Open a Rusty Floodgate
If you have trouble getting started on bite-size brainstorming—you have your PDA stylus in hand, or your fingers poised above your keyboard, but the ideas, or

bites, just don't flow—here are several unblocking techniques used by writers that you can apply to bite-size brainstorming (or for that matter to start anything):

1. Write an e-mail to a friend. Take the pressure off yourself and explain in a letter to a friend what you're trying to do. When you read it back to yourself, nine times out of ten, you've started to list the bites of your elephant. Which brings me to the second unblocking technique . . .

2. Ask a friend to help. If you're having trouble thinking of the bites of your elephant or applying the seat of your pants to the seat of your chair, there's nothing like the support, encouragement and ideas of a family member, close friend, or business colleague. Two or more heads are often better than one.

3. Talk instead of type. Many writers, myself included, admit that when we're "blocked," a reliable alternative to struggling to get the words through our fingers is to talk it out. Speech-recognition software makes this timesaving and *fun*. Speak into a small microphone, and watch your words appear on your screen. More about this in chapter 4.

4. Check for physical stumbling blocks. Review your brainstorming environment; perhaps external, rather than mental, factors are putting up barriers. Have you assembled the necessary brainstorming tools—your PDA with plenty of battery life, your laptop or desktop computer, or pencil and paper? Have you removed yourself from distractions and protected yourself from interruptions?

As with any skill, you'll become more fluent in brainstorming the more you practice. But whether you're a Fortune 500 company determined to double profits in five years or a homemaker intent upon a tidy attic, an entrepreneur who wants to launch a Web site or a family who wants a faster Internet connection, the process of accomplishing the goal begins with brainstorming. And brainstorming consists of the bites of assembling the tools, finding a quiet place, and blocking out some quiet time.

True, you seldom encounter one elephant at a time. In your busy life you often come face-to-face with a stampede of elephants. Lauren M. laughingly recalls, "A therapist friend told us never to undertake too many major life changes at once, but my husband changed jobs, we moved, and I had a baby, all in the same year."

The first step to getting through the stampede, in an e-organized way, is to list the bites of one elephant, then another, then another.

Most productive, e-organized people keep their bite-size brainstorm lists in the to-do list or memo-pad sections of their PDAs so they can refer to them or change them when they need to. When the goal has been accomplished, they take great satisfaction in deleting the lists.

What About the Bites?

"Okay," says Jim B., a busy salesman. "But what's to be done with all the bites?"

Jane Pollak replies, "First you assign deadline dates to each task on your mind map, and then you move those tasks to your calendar. In so doing, you've gone from planning to implementation."

Everyone keeps a calendar these days, and whether you prefer electronic or paper, this is where you record what the experts call "external" appointments—meetings with lawyers, doctors, the PTA, the car mechanic, and so on. They are called external appointments because we are accountable to someone else externally.

Believe it or not, in our incredibly busy lives today, calendars are often underused. They can also serve to remind you of "internal" appointments—that is, the deadlines you set for yourself but for which no one says it must be done today. Many of the bites of your elephants are just such internal appointments because *you* set the deadline. You have made the task a priority and have brought it to your calendar to be done. Writing it down doesn't guarantee that you will do it, but it brings you much closer than just thinking about doing it.

Electronic calendars also let you view a single day, a week, or a month, as you wish. Another very important timesaving feature of your electronic calendar is the repeat function—the ability to enter something once and have it recur daily, weekly, annually, whatever. What's more, repeated calendar appointments don't have to be just meetings with people. You can use them to remind yourself to service your car, pay estimated taxes, or refill vital medical prescriptions. I will discuss specific techniques for making yourself accountable for your internal appointments in chapter 5.

Electronic organizers and PIM software for the desktop feature to-do lists, which you can use to keep track of your miscellaneous tasks that don't belong to a big elephant—for example, call to make an appointment to get your hair cut, pick up your dry cleaning, or mail a check as a memorial gift when someone has died. However, why write or type twice? Save time and put it right into your calendar.

Other Handy Lists

In addition to saving my goal lists, I use the to-do list and memo-pad functions on my PDA to keep track of things I want to remember—books I want to read, videos I want to rent, places I want to visit, restaurants that have been recommended, and so on. At times I will keep a list of "questions for my accountant" or issues to talk over with my doctor, and I often use these functions to build meeting agendas since I'm thinking over several days or weeks of points to discuss. One enterprising dad I know keeps a list of "Kid Quotes," amusing things his two young sons say that he wants to remember. You can create myriad lists to keep track of whatever relates to your life.

Some users keep a list category that they label "pending" for the voice mail or e-mail queries that they send and to which they are waiting for an answer. Or if you have a large contact database, you may want to consider one of the popular CRM software programs, such as ACT! or Goldmine, which have built-in systems where you record what's happened and that remind the user to follow up.

"I would never have guessed how terrific electronic calendars are," exclaims Roslyn Stone Pollock, of Corporate Wellness, Inc., in Mount Kisco, New York. As principal in her family business and a busy mother of two, Roz bought not one but two PDAs, one for herself and one for her husband, Mike.

"I travel for the business; Mike does not," she explains. "Together we keep two calendars—the family's, which includes my airline flight information as well as our son's and daughter's activities, and my business calendar. Thanks to WeSync software on my desktop (www.wesync.com), all we do is click off two boxes, and we have a date on two calendars.

"Before our PDAs, we missed a fair number of things," Roz confesses. "Choir practice, a pickup after a hockey game . . . Now Mike and I are always on the same page. I'm even thinking of buying a PDA for our nanny."

Start at the Finish Line

Writing deadlines in your calendar, and the steps on the way to getting there, prevents what I call "term paper syndrome." Remember when you had a lengthy paper to write and you put it off until the last minute and pulled an all-nighter to get it done on time? Writing the milestones to completing a project in your calendar, spaced out with reasonable time for completion in between, is a sure antidote to all that stress, anxiety, and lack of sleep.

The way to plot the steps in a project, or bites of an elephant, in your calendar is to start at the finish line—that is, write in the deadline—and walk backward. This strategy can be very helpful to people who habitually don't allow enough time for a project.

One woman told me, "It's no wonder I was late to work every morning. I assumed I could put the mail out for the mailman, put the dog in his pen, find my car keys, turn on the security system, run a comb through my hair one last time, find my umbrella, check my briefcase, and lower the thermostat, all in five minutes. It takes me much longer than that to leave the house for the day. Now I plan for these tasks by starting the countdown earlier."

Dual-career couples I've met express frustration that they seldom accomplish everything they want to do on the weekend. When they outline their weekend agendas, I'm aghast at their expectations. They are totally unrealistic. They don't allow for the everyday facts of life that slow them down, like dealing with Saturday traffic, waiting in long lines, running to the bank for more cash, starting a car when the temperature is below zero, and so on. When they go through the exercise of starting at the finish line (the time they want to return home from all their errands) and walking backward, even if they manage only to figure in a reasonable driving time between points, they can reduce their expectations.

Remember the sound advice from Midé Wilkey: "Goals are intended to be read and reviewed regularly so you can sustain your focus on them." Therefore, keep a list of your goals in your PDA, and review it regularly. Written goals save time and help you be more productive.

Chapter 4

You Are an Effective Communicator— Adept at Delegating, Optimizing Meetings, and Minimizing Interruptions

Cynthia S., a home-based graphic designer and mother of two teenage boys, is fed up with interruptions. "Is it too much to ask to have some creative time in which to create?" she asks. "That's what my clients pay me to do, but the only way I can get away from the phone and e-mail is to stay up late or get up very early. My health is starting to suffer."

Jared T. is drowning in his e-mail. As a salesman for a travel tour company and a weekend football coach, he's away from his desk more than he's at it. One well-meaning colleague suggests, "Get unified messaging," while another says, "You're not using the tools you've got. Use those filters." Jared would be happy just to get through his inbox more often than every two weeks.

Maureen W. confesses that morale is very low in her department at the village hall. "We waste so much time in meetings," she says. "Nothing is ever accomplished." Her boss will be attending leadership training, and Maureen has her fingers crossed that he'll learn some skills that everyone can benefit from. "I know I have lots of room for improvement in running meetings for my church and the PTA."

*   *   *

There's no denying that our many technologies have brought us increased connectivity. We read of the "Evernet," the ability to be on-line all the time from everywhere. However, as I wrote in the introduction, ability does not necessarily equal desirability! Effective communicators know how to *disconnect* when they need to—to avoid interruptions in their creative or recreation time. As a time-management expert, I know one immutable fact: One hour of focused time is worth more than two hours with interruptions. I want to be connected, but on *my* terms.

In addition, effective communicators know how to create more time for themselves by delegating effectively— by passing on assignments to others in a way that ensures they are completed on time and in full. And finally, they don't waste participants' time in meetings. Instead, they know how to maximize time spent when they bring people together to accomplish specific goals.

Just as no one is *born* organized, no one is born knowing how to save time in written and spoken communications. Like lifetime learning habits, communicating to save time—either by writing or by speaking—is a set of skills that is acquired through practice. In the ideal scenario, you decide to learn tennis, for example, and then have some lessons and commit to practicing. Your improved tennis playing is self-reinforcing: It's so personally satisfying to see your own progress that you play more and continue to enjoy your development at tennis. The same goes for communicating.

With more and more demands on our time from increased communications, it is more essential than ever that we speak and write clearly and succinctly. True, people don't *listen* as effectively as they should, but as communicators, we can go a long way toward saving time and improving productivity if we practice certain communications skills and adopt productive behaviors.

E-mail Productivity

When Steve White, principal of Growth Communications, in Norwalk, Connecticut (www.growthcommunications. com), told me that he seldom has any e-mails in his e-mail cache, I looked at him incredulously. As the owner of a thriving e-sales and marketing business, how would he not be barraged by e-mails? Everyone else I know is.

Steve uses Microsoft Outlook for his e-mail program and takes liberal advantage of the menu choice "Organize." Like many similar applications, this function in Outlook allows Steve to file his e-mail before he reads it. He has created "Rules" based on whom the e-mail is from. Steve's customized e-mail folders, according to his rules, are lined up vertically on the left of his screen. He knows that he has new e-mail whenever a folder appears darker.

"These folders are ideal for holding electronic newsletters, which arrive at regular intervals, as well as correspondence from specific clients, friends, or family," Steve explains. "For people who have multiple e-mail addresses, they can establish a rule, or folder, for each address."

It is also possible to establish a rule that will reduce "spam," or junk e-mails. Charles Asmar (www.highest-rank.com), instructs Outlook or Outlook Express users as follows: "When selecting your Conditions and Actions, specify any e-mail where the 'To' line does *not* contain your specific address. Then select 'Delete.' If this first filter doesn't catch an unwanted message, try right clicking on the message and selecting Block Sender."

You will save time by organizing your e-mails before you read them, but what about additional techniques for stemming their tide overall? Here are several suggestions gleaned from on-line tips:

- Ask to be removed from the distribution list. Politely ask your friends to cease sending jokes, chain letters, and the like.

- Many on-line e-tailers let you "opt out" of being solicited based on your previous purchases. If the site sends out commercial messages, you should be given a choice whether you want to receive e-mail from them or from their third-party partners. If you don't want their notices, be sure to check the "No" box.

- For announcements from e-tailers, unsolicited newsletters, and other intrusions, Internet watchdogs advise that you *not* follow the "remove" instructions at the bottom of the document. (This tells the perpetrator that your address is valid and that you read your mail.) Instead, use your DELETE key.

- What about the Web sites that require you to "register" to use their services? Before you do, read their privacy policy to see how it uses your personal information. (Some users choose *never* to register on-line for anything as a means of reducing spam. For me, that's extreme. If I download free software, for example, I want the site to know that I am a user in the likely event that I will contact them for tech support. However, I always check the "No" box when asked if I want to receive additional "news" or product information.)

- Have a private e-mail box and reveal it to a small inner circle of contacts. You should have this especially if you regularly visit chat rooms, or if your address is posted at on-line discussion groups or on Web sites. Spammers buy lists of e-mail addresses or use special software that mines addresses from the Internet.

- Use spam filters. Many e-mail programs have built-in tools that block messages sent from certain addresses or that filter messages based on key words that you define. Check the on-line help files for your e-mail software.

- To opt out of AOL (America Online) partner e-mailings and other marketing junk, go to Keyword: Choices. This will bring you to the Marketing Preferences Control Panel, where you can set your preferences for receiving mail, telephone calls, e-mail, and pop-up advertising. Check these settings periodically because AOL's policy is to reset these to the defaults after about a year.

- For additional suggestions on how to stop the spread of spam, check out the helpful hints at www.learnthenet.com.

Unfortunately, our world of increased access has created increased expectations. When giving keynote speeches, I've been known to ask my audience, "Are you 911?" They look at me as if to say, "Well, of course, I'm not 911. Who's she kidding?" But on pushing a little harder, I ask if, in responding to their e-mails and phone calls, they *behave* as if they had to reply immediately twenty-four hours a day. Invariably, I hear murmurs of self-recognition and uncomfortable shifting in their chairs. This from the same people who complain they have no time! Think about what you're *communicating* when you answer an e-mail right away.

When should you process your e-mail? The answer depends on the demands of your work and on your lifestyle. For those who live their lives in e-mail—on-line customer-service reps, for example—the answer is "all the time." If your work and lifestyle are of a different nature, then you have some options.

Many people I surveyed said they answer e-mail typically three times a day, including on their home computers after work outside the home. Still others—permanently attached to their two-way pagers—insist *they're more productive* by answering e-mail in snatches of time, like Sarah W. in chapter 2.

"Who says you have to answer all your e-mail in one day?" asks Toni M., a cavalier writing colleague of mine. "Did you ever do that with your regular mail?" As one who sorts *but seldom acts on* a piece of snail mail on the same day I receive it, I have to admit she has a point.

I use my e-mail's "automatic signature" function to communicate my response time. To those to whom I write, the end of an e-mail reads: "Please note: I answer e-mail once a day at the end of the day." This is followed by all my contact information. Bottom line: If it's urgent, call me on the telephone. (Are there exceptions to this message? Absolutely. In fact, I have *four* customized signatures that I use, depending on the situation.)

I recall a college professor's auto reply that I encountered a year ago: "I receive up to 200 e-mails every day. I try to answer them all, but seldom in less than six weeks' time. I appreciate your patience." I have no idea if his count was true, but he certainly caused me to adjust my expectations, and eventually, I received his answer to my query.

Another outgoing e-mail tip is to use "auto responders," or automatic answers to all, or certain, incoming e-mails while you're away or otherwise unavailable. These are not only good e-mail etiquette, but again, they communicate realistic *expectations*, and clear, concise communications save time.

As one who, on most days, answers e-mail "once a day at the end of the day," I have disabled the e-mail icon that notifies me of an incoming message. I don't need that cerebral interruption while I'm working on more important priorities. On the other hand, I receive a lot of customized e-mail at regular intervals—some once a day; others once a week or once a month—thanks to Microsoft's Active Desktop (see chapter 2), as well as Thefetcher.com (www. thefetcher.com), which e-mails some of my favorite Web pages every morning.

Lead by Example

In addition to using your application's automatic signature and auto reply functions, Abby Marks-Beale, owner of The Reading Edge in Wallingford, Connecticut (www.the-reading-edge.com), offers these suggestions for e-mail productivity:

"Don't underestimate the importance of a good subject line," she advises. "Imagine that you had to boil down your message to a three- to five-word nugget, such as 'new expense report policy effect immed'ly,' 'need reply before Fri,' 'option to renew expires 3/1.' " I, too, recommend that an expiration date appear in the Subject line whenever possible. It saves time if you tell your reader how important the message is and when you expect a reply.

In terms of the body of the e-mail, "Think postcard, not letter," says Abby. "Another way to determine the importance of brevity is to imagine how you would behave if e-mail wasn't free and if you paid by the word." What a sobering thought! And surely enough to raise our collective consciousness to *keep it short*.

A few of my regular e-mail correspondents have requested that instead of sending attachments, I paste the document into the e-mail, and I willingly comply. In this age of "permission marketing"—that is, selling to people who give you electronic go-ahead—a cardinal rule is to deliver the message in the format that the (potential) buyer requests. Think about it: If, as a public relations consultant, I approach a TV producer by phone when she prefers a fax, or if I send a fax to an editor who explicitly desires e-mail, what a complete waste of time! I store these media preferences in my ACT! database, along with the quirks and penchants of my friends and family.

Another way you can *lead by example* is when forwarding an e-mail do your recipients a favor and delete all the distribution lists that clog the beginnings of so many e-mails. "My enthusiasm for reading the e-mail diminishes by how long it takes me to scroll to find the actual message," says James E., a high school English teacher and advisor to the school newspaper. "And I'm trying to pass along my reactions to my students so they learn the wisdom of brevity."

If you are e-organized, you know how to send an e-mail to a list of recipients using the "blind copy" function—that is, send it so that your receivers don't have to scroll through an often-lengthy distribution list. In AOL version 6.0, for example, users should type their own e-mail address in the "To" window and paste their distribution list of addresses, enclosed in parentheses and separated by commas, into the "cc" window. Then click "Send." It's that simple, and yet I know very few who practice this courteous and timesaving technique.

Jeff C., who "lives" on-line all day in his job as a customer-service rep for a watch company, recommends this processing shortcut for answering people's e-mail queries: "I use the 'include the original in replies' feature in my e-mail program's settings. Then I click Reply and answer their questions IN CAPS. Customers' questions and the reps' replies go into a permanent record. This is one way our company audits our service." Jeff has brought this simple, timesaving technique to his personal correspondence as well. "I find people appreciate my repeating their questions followed by specific answers right beneath them." *Appreciate* is the key word here. Your friends might prefer that you keep your e-mail replies brief.

One last, but *important*, admonishment about replying to e-mail. It saves time, and reduces anxiety on the part of the sender, when you "close the loop"—that is, acknowledge that you received the note. E-mail is not perfect, and sometimes my missives can get lost in cyberspace. Therefore, I'm grateful when recipients reply with a simple "okay," "got it," or "done."

Another popular way to use e-mail, and to avoid having to buy and send a card, is to send electronic greetings. Opportunities to choose and customize e-cards, as well as invitations, abound on the Web. Their "intangibilities" are not without their detractors, but personally, I enjoy receiving them. And their use is not limited to birthdays and anniversaries. As one who believes firmly that praise, kudos, and congratulations *in any form* save time by improving morale, I invite you to check out the praise-filled offerings at:

- Blue Mountain (www.bluemountain.com)
- Amazon.com (www.amazon.com)
- Yahoo! Greetings (http://greetings.yahoo.com/)
- #1 Online Greeting Cards (www.1onlinegreetingcards.com)
- Hallmark (www.hallmark.com)

Want to send an e-card from "all of you" as a group? Group Cards (www.groupcards.com) can help. And for environmentalist readers, or those who actively want to contribute to "saving trees," the Center for a New American Dream (http://www.simplifytheholidays.org/) is a nonprofit site that uses children's artwork for e-cards.

If you work for a large company, you probably receive notice of important meetings via software programs like Microsoft Outlook. For your personal life, or for those without access to these resources after hours, you can take advantage of free sites that help you plan and announce meetings or events, such as Yahoo! Groups (http://groups.yahoo.com/local/news.html) and Evite.com (www.evite.com).

And while we're talking about e-mail, should you select a free e-mail supplier like Yahoo, Hotmail, and others, or the commercial e-mail available through your ISP (Internet service provider), such as AOL or Earthlink? Many who strive to be very e-organized assume that they should choose only one service for the sake of simplicity.

In principle, I would agree, but in fact, I interviewed many individuals who extol the benefits of *managing* their e-mail by using two or more accounts.

Paul S., a manufacturers rep who travels a lot, swears by his free Web-based e-mail account for several reasons: "My e-mail is available from any Web-enabled computer anywhere in the world, without configuration hassles or long-distance costs. Furthermore, my free account is permanent, whereas my company-supplied e-mail has changed three times since I joined up. Also, I feel I have more privacy with Web-based e-mail than I have with my company's program. And finally, my service offers a wide selection of domain names so I've selected two different addresses for two different spheres of my life." That's certainly one way to do it.

Free e-mail is *everywhere* on the Web, but there are several ISPs (Internet service providers) that also offer free Internet access, as well as free e-mail. For example:

- Netzero (www.netzero.com)
- Lycos (www.lycos.com)
- AvantGo (www.avantgo.com)
- Excite (www.excite.com)

For a free ISP (Internet service provider) comparison chart, check out Dailyedeals.com (http://www.dailyedeals.com/free_internet/free_isp.htm).

In fairness, several geek pals have cautioned me on free suppliers, believing them to be slower and less reliable than standard commercial accounts. And many readers will remember what happened to Microsoft's Hotmail system in August of 1999 when they discovered a security flaw that left millions of accounts vulnerable to unauthorized access. In addition, these free services are allowed to reserve a section of your browser *at all times* for showing ads. This is much of what slows down the service and can be very annoying when it takes up an already precious amount of your screen space.

But Paul S. insists, "Free e-mail is definitely a useful complement to business e-mails, especially for someone like me who travels worldwide." However, he does recommend that for better and safer use, we should clear out our e-mail caches whenever we use public-access computers.

Christopher Pankratz, Web Development Engineer for Computer Consulting Associates (www.ccaii.com), says we should be especially careful with free Internet access in many airports in the United States and abroad. "I urge all my friends to clear the cache—or in Microsoft Internet Explorer, go to 'Internet Options,' and perform 'Delete Files' and 'Clear History'—for the maximum in privacy. Then close the browser. This way the next guy after you can't come in, hit the Back button and read your e-mails."

Another popular feature of e-mail programs is instant messaging, which enables private, person-to-person live chats with any or all of the people you've listed in your address book (sometimes called a "buddy list"). Whenever your buddies are on-line at the same time you are, the instant messaging software alerts you so you can chat back and forth using pop-up dialog boxes. Free messaging tools include:

- AOL's Instant Messenger, or AIM (www.aol.com)
- ICQ (http://web.icq.com)
- MSN Messenger (http://messenger.msn.com)
- Yahoo! Messenger (http://messenger.yahoo.com)

In spite of the advantages, these applications have interoperability issues—that is, you have to have the same software as your friends in order to chat with them. In addition, you'll probably be happier if you set your software so that you have to approve users, most often established by choosing Preferences from the setup menu.

In discussions of e-mail etiquette, instant messaging has its proponents and detractors. Personally, I resent its intrusion and disable my software unless, of course, I have *scheduled* an on-line discussion, which I frequently do. I know four sisters who planned a fiftieth wedding anniversary party for their parents by instant messaging, as well as some very computer-savvy senior citizens who arranged events for their fifty-fifth college reunion with e-mail "conferencing." Again, if you're proactive, these tools can contribute to your productivity.

Entire books have been devoted to e-mail. Suffice it to say, it's a powerful tool that can save time and money, but it can also *take over* your time and waste money in your lost productivity. The point is to *manage* it— don't let it manage you. EMailman.com (www.emailman. com) is a free one-stop source for solving electronic-mail problems. Helpful advice is also available from Mary Houten-Kemp's Everything E-mail (www.everything-email.com).

Telephone Productivity

No contest—people's number one telephone complaint is telemarketing calls. To remove your name from the callers' lists, write to the Telephone Preference Service, Direct Marketing Association, Dept. P, P.O. Box 9014,

Farmingdale, NY 11735-9014. Include your name, address, and phone number. Remember, just as for reducing junk (paper) mail, it takes up to six months before the full effects will be felt.

In addition, some states now have laws that require telemarketers to consult a "no-call list." If your name is on it, they are not supposed to contact you. My home state of Connecticut passed such a law, which became effective 1 January 2001, and residents can add their name by writing to the Department of Consumer Protection, Trade Practices Division, 165 Capitol Ave., Hartford, CT 06106. The telephone number is 800-842-2679, the fax is 860-713-7239, and the Web site is http://www.state.ct.us/dcp/nocall.htm. Using the same e-mail formula as Connecticut's—that is, the state's two-letter abbreviation following "state"—I was able to find other states' Web sites on the Internet. Searching on "consumer protection" brought up instructions for adding my name to the telemarketing no-call list, if the state has such a law.

Telecommunications consultants frequently tout the timesaving benefits of caller-ID service, which can block calls from anonymous numbers. The caller will be told to identify his number or call back from a different phone. Many anonymous callers are telemarketers.

The second most frequent complaint I hear about telephone use is toward callers who perpetuate "telephone tag," or the lengthy cycle of voice mails that accomplishes nothing. Telephone productivity is increased when callers actually imagine that they will *never* talk live. In other words, pretend you're only going to communicate by voice mail, but you have to move your agenda forward.

After using this technique, Karen R., a recruiter, exclaims, "It's amazing how detailed and specific my voice mails became! I have to describe job positions and tell potential candidates about interviews, as well as describe the candidates to my client employers and set up interviews. I would say ninety-five percent of my communication is by voice mail."

You can give callers a hint or two in the outgoing voice instruction on *your* phone. For example, when I leave a voice mail, I always tell the receiver when I'll be available to receive their return call. Likewise, I instruct callers to tell me when is the best time to reach them by phone. And as one who makes liberal use of telephone appointments, I also invite callers to suggest a time slot in which we can talk live for a specific amount of time.

For individuals and families with only one line for the telephone and the Internet, services like Callwave.com (www.callwave.com) and Pagoo.com (www.pagoo.com) let you know when there's an incoming call. You can disconnect and take the call, or it will take a message. More and more local telephone service providers are offering these services, as well.

Finally, telephone productivity is enhanced when the caller reaches his party live and politely asks, "Is this a good time to talk?" If it's not convenient, chances are very good that the receiver will be willing to schedule a later appointment.

Conversely, if you answer a phone call but don't have time to talk (and part of me asks, with answering machines and voice-mail systems, why you answered in the first place), offer the caller an alternative: "Sorry, Art. I can't talk now, but I'm available after four-thirty." Remember, you haven't said no to Art; you've only said, "Not now."

Consolidating Messages

In chapter 1, I discussed cell-phone service options, including Simulring (www.simulring.com), which rings on up to three lines even though your friends and family can call just one local phone number.

Another timesaving option for *you*, the message receiver, is a "unified messaging service"—also called "all-in-one communications" and "personal communications hub"—which allows you to manage all your messages—e-mail, fax, and voice mail—via a single inbox. For the greatest flexibility, you want to be able to retrieve your messages *both* by phone and by e-mail on your PC, laptop, or PDA.

Web-based products, like Voicecom (www.voicecom. com), uReach (www.ureach.com) and Unified Messaging (www.unified-messaging.com), deliver your voice mail directly to your e-mail in box and to the phone number you select. They'll take calls for you when your phone is busy, while you're on-line and when you're away. When someone leaves you a message, the service will alert you via e-mail, pager, or cell phone. You get free access to your messages from anywhere in the world via the Web or via one toll-free number. And you can also leave a personal greeting letting your callers know you're not able to answer their call.

It's important to note that, while unified messaging contributes significantly to e-organization, not all systems perform the same functions, and there is also a wide range in pricing. Many plans offer free sign-up and a demo, a great way to test a program yourself. Also, beware of these limitations:

- If you want e-mail messages to be included in your unified in box, know that some plans require that you use certain e-mail providers.
- Not every service is capable of text-to-speech technology, so you won't always have the option of listening to your e-mail or faxes over the phone.
- Most Web-based services are paid each month, but before signing up, make sure you can cancel your service without penalties at any time.
- When registering for a free service, find out if the number you call to retrieve your messages is toll-free.
- Determine if you'll have to listen to any advertisements before you get your messages by phone.
- Find out if you can use your existing e-mail address as your e-mail inbox. If you must create another address, this could defeat the purpose of "unified messaging."
- What happens with attachments? Can you attach a fax in your inbox to an e-mail message and forward it?
- A key question: How long will it take for a message to be moved to your in box?

These all-in-one communications services are becoming increasingly popular. Many users become convinced of their value while on the job and want to bring the convenience home to their families. Some plans are geared especially to the needs of small businesses. Extra features and options are being added all the time, and increased competition has made them very affordable. To keep current on this growing trend, visit the very helpful news and information portal, Unified Messaging (www.unified-messaging.com).

Speech-Activated Systems

One of the most advanced features you can add to your unified messaging service is voice recognition. "When I'm out on sales calls, I don't have a PC nearby, and I have no patience for trying to type on my cell phone's keypad," says Ben T., an engineer. "My all-in-one service allows me to retrieve my messages by voice commands. I can even answer my e-mails by dictating a reply. This added service contributes tremendously to my productivity."

Ben's enthusiasm is not unique. AOL members have signed up in droves for AOLbyPhone (www.aol.com), one of several new "voice portals" whose recorded voices read small nuggets of on-line information to callers in response to set spoken commands. Other telephone-based portals for individuals to consider are:

- Hey Anita (www.heyanita.com)—a toll-free phone number provides Internet-based information—including stock quotes, news, weather, sports reports—through a series of voice prompts.
- Tellme.com (www.tellme.com) also gives you information, preferences for which you set up on the Internet, over the phone—stock quotes, news, weather—from one toll-free number.
- Virtual Advisor (www.onstar.com), a driver-oriented service that provides the latest audio news from the *Wall Street Journal Online*.

There are many other companies that are developing "carrier-grade" voice portals, which will be marketed to you through your land-line, cell-phone and PDA service plans.

While we're talking about receiving your e-mail by voice, it's important not to pass over the extraordinary timesaving attributes of speech recognition software for creating written documents. Did you know that you can now speak instead of type and watch your words appear on your computer's screen? You can dictate your e-mail, as well as letters, memos, proposals, and yes, even book chapters.

I first became acquainted with digital (no audio cassettes!) dictation when I decided to give a try to Point & Speak offered in a banner ad from AOL. At $39.95 with a thirty-day trial, what did I have to lose? And now I'm hooked, big-time. So far I've managed to avoid the dreaded side-effect of my profession—carpal tunnel syndrome— but I've endured a nasty case of tennis elbow. However, these days I don't fear its return: I spend more time talking than typing.

As terrific as it is, digital dictation does not excuse you from maintaining a careful editor's eye. But after you train the software to recognize your speech patterns, it's amazingly accurate. What's more, when you're away from your desktop, it's possible to dictate into a voice recorder and then download your spoken words later. Some recorders, like the Olympus DS-150, the Sony ICD-MS1 VTP, and the Sanyo ICR B100, come bundled with the software. For less expensive recorders, you have to install the software on your desktop separately.

Allison Z. is a busy medical writer, mother, and grandmother who frequently dictates follow-up e-mails into her voice recorder. "It works like this," she explains. "After I've met face-to-face with a magazine editor about an assignment, I speak a follow-up e-mail into my voice recorder, confirming our agreement—topics covered, primary sources, word length, delivery date, and fee—while I commute home on the train. When I get home, I download the dictation for automatic transcription. I've also dictated some questions that I want to ask those primary sources, while they're fresh in my mind. I make sure I launch this e-mail from the editor's record in my CRM program, so I have a permanent, electronic 'trail.' " When I asked Allison why she didn't just type those e-mails and memos into a two-way pager or other PDA, she replied, "I'd rather talk than type." Amen.

Many a gadget guru with whom I spoke longs to be able to dictate into his PDA. The biggest challenge is that dictation software typically requires 128 megabytes of memory and an 800-megahertz processor. ScanSoft, for one, has a new speech system for navigating handheld computers. However, "it is expected that dictation speech recognition on palm-top devices will supplement, rather than replace, speech recognition by desktop and laptop computers," according to Peter Fleming, a speech-recognition consultant. "That having been said," he adds, "dictation speech recognition, in its present form on desktop and laptop computers, is an eminently usable, potential productivity-enhancing technology whose time has arrived."

Speech recognition software has progressed along a bumpy road, and the software vendors are down to two— IBM's ViaVoice and ScanSoft's NaturallySpeaking—but I (and many writers I know) love mine. For more information on voice recorders and speech recognition software, check out the database of helpful articles in *Speech Technology Magazine* (www.speechtek.com).

Save Time by Delegating

We can achieve more time for our most important priorities by using timesaving techniques for e-mail, telephone use, unified messaging, and digital dictation. We can also capture more time by delegating to others. Leaders from many spheres of life—from the scions of industry to grassroots community organizers—know how to delegate successfully. Delegation works when assigned work gets done on time and correctly. In fact, at the top of my list of life's biggest wastes of time and annoyances is *reverse* delegation—when a job I've assigned comes back incomplete or done incorrectly. Then it invariably ends up being me who has to backfill and do it right. *What a colossal waste of time and resources!*

Everyone knows the first two steps of delegation:

1. Describe the job.
2. State the deadline for completion.

However, untrained delegators frequently stop here. In fact, the two most important pieces of information have not yet been communicated. They are:

3. Say why you chose this individual for the task.
4. State how you define success. Say what successful completion looks like.

With step 3, you have an opportunity to "stroke" the person. For example, "Rick, you're the perfect guy for this project. Look what a great job you did at the conference last year. I know our multimedia displays are going to be even better this time with you at the helm." In step 4, Rick's boss spells out exactly how he wants the displays—

what size screens they will need, how long various video segments will run, how interactive he hopes they will be, and so on.

These four steps work equally well on the home front. Here's a true story. One summer day I had delegated sweeping out the garage to my then-preteen son. I said, "Please get it done before dark." So much for steps 1 and 2.

That evening I inspected his work, and much to my dismay, I found many leaves still strewn about the floor. Now mind you, I wasn't looking to perform surgery on my garage floor, but I did expect that the leaves would have been swept up. My lesson—from hindsight, I realize I had neglected steps 3 and 4. I could have said, "You're a valuable member of our family team and I'm counting on your help today. Please sweep out the garage before dark. And by the way, a clean garage means there are no leaves or other debris left on the floor."

A complaint I hear often comes from Natalie M., an administrative assistant: "I'm the person who *receives* the delegation in my office, and yet my bosses *never* tell me how they want something done." To Natalie, I reply, "*Demand* to know."

I, too, have had bosses like Natalie has. After having to redo tasks because I wasn't given clear directions, I screwed up my courage and said something like, "Excuse me. I need just a minute of your time. For these proposals for tomorrow's meeting, do you want them double spaced? Should there be a cover page? What should it say? Should I put the proposals in folders? How many extra copies will you need? Who will want electronic copies?" And so on.

If you use technology to delegate—e-mail, voice mail, or group conferencing—you will save time and reduce the possibility to having to start again, if you communicate all four pieces of information.

Virtual Assistants

In my professional life, I network with a large number of entrepreneurs; many are writers, speakers, and consultants like me. A growing trend that I observe is how many of us delegate to "virtual assistants"—independent contractors who provide administrative support or specialized business services from a distance. Thanks to modern communications through the Internet, fax, and telephone, my assistant doesn't have to work in my office. Instead she works wherever and whenever she chooses, as long as she completes my to-dos on time. It's more *productive* for me to work on my top priorities and delegate the rest to my VA.

"My VA lives a thousand miles away from me, and I couldn't survive without her," says David L., a consultant to the travel industry. "She maintains my calendar and my contact database, which we both access from the Web, and does all my e-mailings, invoicing, and bookkeeping. We're in touch by phone and e-mail, and I always know where she is on her list of tasks because that's stored on the Web and accessed by both of us, too." Clearly David has found a system of delegating that works for him.

Providing virtual assistance is a burgeoning home-based business category nationally and internationally. "VAs can help a company that needs extra people to meet seasonal demands; provide unique skills for a special project; or step in to meet the demands of business growth, locally, domestically or globally," says the International Virtual Assistants Association (www.ivaa.org). Additional resources are available from AssistU (www.assistu.com), which provides training, coaching, and referral, and Staff-centrix (www.staffcentrix.com), which has compiled a listing of all virtual assistants who have passed the Ethics-Check.com examination.

While technology has made virtual assistance possible, it has not removed the necessity for clear communications. In fact, precise directions to your assistant, without the benefit of "face time," are more necessary than ever. The four steps of delegation still apply:

1. Describe the job.
2. State the deadline for completion.
3. Say why you chose this individual for the task.
4. State how you define success. Say what successful completion looks like.

Maximize Meetings

Effective communicators know how to manage their tele-communications and how to delegate to achieve the results they desire. They also know how to maximize meetings, whether they are virtual, as in audio and video conferencing, or in person. Unfortunately, the biggest complaint I hear from employees is that most meetings waste their time and beat down their morale. Similarly, community volunteers grumble loudly that church and civic meetings run too long and don't accomplish enough. And family meetings around the dinner table can disintegrate quickly unless *listening* is a huge part of the equation. What's to be done?

Meeting planning is the subject of entire books, but the fact is, we all know when we've been to a good one: Participants are smiling, they feel inspired, and they understand their marching orders for the next meeting. I've often seen thanks and congratulations offered to the leaders. The *good vibes* are palpable, and participants depart feeling as if they've just experienced an excellent use of their time.

How can you plan meetings that don't waste time? "Whether it's a live meeting or a form of teleconferencing, circulate a detailed agenda beforehand," says Russ C., the director of communications for a hospital.

"If you struggle to start your meetings on time, and your participants routinely straggle in, put a period of time for schmoozing at the top of the agenda. In other words, let people see that from eight-forty-five to nine o'clock, for example, they can come in, take their coats off, grab a cup of coffee, ask about your weekend, and so on. But at nine o'clock the gavel comes down."

I feel that meetings are a valuable use of time if they solicit feedback or generate new ideas. Roxanne C., a director of human resources, agrees: "Whenever I convene department heads to brainstorm solutions to problems, large or small, I find that one plus one plus one always equals more than three. I mean, you can *feel* the exponential synergy when people are working together.

"Don't call a meeting just to pass along information," she adds. "You can do that electronically or one-on-one."

Vince D., a sales manager, says, "The most important reason to bring several people together is to make them *accountable* to each other—everyone has some results to report—all in the process of reaching a team goal." Vince should know. His sales team for an international sporting goods company is always the leader for contracts signed and billed.

A successful meeting, then, is one in which each participant goes away with a new assignment that carries the project another step further. As Vince points out, "When the meeting adjourns, everyone must know what's expected of him or her for the next gathering."

Have you ever attended meetings in which the conversation deviates away from the agenda? I'm sure we all have. And the detour can be very frustrating for anyone who doesn't have unlimited time to spend on the diversion, let alone the meeting itself.

"I've been there!" says Sharon L., who works with hospital volunteers. "I find the surest antidotes to falling off the agenda track are a firm hand on the gavel and the courage to say, 'In the interest of time, I have to table this discussion until our next meeting.' Sometimes I also ask a subcommittee to investigate the issue and draft a policy for future consideration. Either way I send a message to the diverters that their issue is important, just not right now."

And speaking of courage, the most effective meeting leaders I've observed are brave enough to ask participants to fill out an evaluation. "Whether we meet in person, or more often by audio-teleconference, immediately afterwards every participant receives an e-mail from me asking, *Was today's meeting a good use of your time?*" Russ explains. "They are instructed to reply to my assistant, who compiles the evaluations anonymously, and then passes them to me. And I often learn something worthwhile from their comments."

Whether you're working as a community volunteer, as a department head in a large corporation, or one-on-one with your virtual assistant, meetings will be more productive if you practice these timesaving techniques:

1. Distribute an agenda beforehand.
2. Include at the top of the agenda time for convening and mingling.
3. Start on time.
4. Minimize agenda detours by "tabling" discussions or assigning them to subcommittees.
5. Make sure all participants leave knowing what they're responsible for at the next meeting.
6. Adjourn on time.

Chapter 5

You Have a System for Personal Accountability—You Know How to Make Good on Your Good Intentions

*For eight years, **Eric V.** has been a stay-at-home dad for his two daughters, while his wife, Annette, works full-time as an attorney. Both daughters have been in school all day for a year now, and Eric had planned to resume his work as a fitness trainer, but there's always something that gets in the way—the car has to go into the shop, his daughters have dentist appointments, the refrigerator is leaking, and so on. Eric has thought about his goals and done bite-size brainstorms, but he's stuck in first gear.*

__Sandra B.__, who with her husband owns a day spa, has discovered the joys of e-organization. She regularly visits a local computer store to check out the latest gadgets and enhancements and has started receiving two on-line newsletters on wireless communications. In addition, she has purchased a handheld PDA, and her e-coach is showing her how to take advantage of her e-mail's organizing capabilities. She's even signed up with a unified messaging service. But something's falling through the cracks: Sandra isn't moving ahead on plans for her Web site, nor is she taking full advantage of her new CRM software. As she examines her electronic calendar, she sees many tasks scheduled but not accomplished.

Robert U., a software developer, cries, "I have no life!"
For four years he has worked long hours and banked a
lot of money, but he's taken only two vacations, both of
them to family weddings. He was captain of the golf team
in college but hasn't swung a club in years. He also en-
joyed kayaking as an undergraduate; now he can't tell
you where the nearest body of water is. Balance is what
Robert's longing for. "I need time away from my com-
puter, my PDA, and my cell. I'm the head of my depart-
ment. How do I disconnect?"

Getting It Done, Period

Several years ago after I had concluded a keynote speech
about saving time and getting organized, a gentleman
raised his hand to ask a question.

"Yes, sir?" I called out to where he sat in the back of
the room.

The man stood and said in a deep Southern drawl,
"Ma'am, I think everything you've said tonight is just
wonderful, and I'm imagining all the ways I can apply
your suggestions to my life. But what's to prevent everything you've said from evaporating between here and my
car in the parking lot?"

"Mister," I replied, "I am *so* glad you asked that question. Indeed, how do we make good on our good intentions?" And I proceeded to answer his question.

In the preceding chapters, I have documented the many
benefits of getting e-organized:

- By practicing lifetime learning habits, you'll keep
  current on technology trends at *your* pace.

- By having a system for processing and storing documents, you'll know where to find things.
- By writing goals, breaking them down into smaller bites, and entering them into your calendar, you'll have a written plan for where you're going and when you'll get there.
- By adopting timesaving communications strategies, you'll be connected on *your* terms.

However, as you have read in the examples at the beginning of this chapter, it's a fantasy to believe that if you're e-organized, everything will just happen. In fact, there's a missing piece—the most important piece of all—accountability. The experts know that time management is common sense in theory and self-discipline in practice. Happily, there are techniques for enhancing self-discipline. Chapter 5 will guide you through the steps for *getting it done, period.*

When I first committed to writing this book, I confess I confronted daily attacks of doubt and panic. I was confident in my ability as a writer and as an expert in organization and saving time, but *technology*? Help! I don't have a degree in computer science. I can read up and study it, but where do I stop? And how will I deal with the proverbial fire hose of constant change in technology innovation?

I make my living as a writer, in several forms, so backing out was not an option, however tempting. Instead, I took a deep breath and decided to practice the advice that I preach. After all, I thought, using technology is just a set of skills—like driving a car. And as my friend Brad Fisher says, "You don't have to know how the car works. You just have to know how to drive the car." So I set about writing a plan and then writing the book.

The way to make yourself accountable, to *get it done*, *period*, is to tell someone what you're going to do, on a regular basis, and then show them that you've done it. The chapters of this book were completed because I meet regularly with three other nonfiction authors to read aloud and critique each other. I wouldn't think of showing up empty-handed. How embarrassing!

As I mentioned in chapter 3, there are basically just two kinds of calendar entries—*external* appointments and *internal* appointments. By external, I mean doctors, lawyers, bosses, clients, friends, spouses, kids—anyone to whom you are responsible externally on a specific date, at a particular time. Nine times out of ten you meet your obligations to others. You don't like to let people down, your livelihood depends on it, you care what other people think, and so on.

Internal appointments, on the other hand, are the commitments you make to yourself but for which there is no higher authority saying, "This must be done today or else." The goal-setting process directs you to bring the bites of your goals into your calendar, which means you have identified a block of free time in which to accomplish this internal task. However, being human, you frequently sabotage your own good intentions—something else gets in the way, you "don't feel like doing it," a more urgent priority comes up, for example. At the end of the day or the week or the month, like Sandra, you look at your calendar pages and find your internal to-dos undone.

The surefire antidote to procrastination, getting sidetracked, running out of gas—whatever you want to call it—is to join a group of like-minded individuals, state your goals out loud, and deliver your results to the group.

This is one of the reasons that executive coaching has caught on so phenomenally—people are realizing that they need support, advice, and someone to *insist* that they be accountable.

"Thanks to my executive coach, I have doubled my revenue," says Gus R., an insurance agent. "She helped me articulate precise goals and develop specific actions to achieve them. I couldn't have done it alone."

Accountability Groups

A group forum for accountability is sometimes called a Mastermind Group. Many parents, entrepreneurs, artists, employees, inventors, writers, and just plain folks who want to live proactively participate in groups like these where, under the direction of a facilitator, members go around the circle and state what they've accomplished since their last meeting. Next, everyone in turn shares the obstacles or personal logjams that they encountered, followed by suggestions from the others on how to refocus and recommit. Finally, each person reveals for these witnesses what specific tasks they will complete before the next Mastermind session. The next meeting, then, becomes the *external* deadline for finishing what they've committed to, and each one is accountable to all of the other individuals in the group.

Are there ever group dropouts? Of course there are. But the vast majority of participants keep showing up, continue finishing their tasks, and maintain their self-discipline, one task at a time, for the simple reason that there's a whole other group of people who are showing up, too. Spirits are buoyed and morale is boosted by members' triumphs. Success is contagious!

Barbara R., a special events planner, credits her increased success to the advice, wisdom, and support of her Mastermind Group. "In the early innings I was floundering. I hadn't defined my special strengths, nor my target market. After just five months, I have a business plan and marketing materials. I'm on my way!"

A more personal form of support has produced measurable results for Kim D., a stay-at-home mom and community volunteer. "The stress level in my home has been reduced by half since I joined a parents support group, available through my local PTA. We have a trained facilitator, and our focus is on the specific actions we can take to reverse our children's undesirable behaviors. There are still lots of areas to work on, but we're really *there* for each other, and it's clear that we're obligated to attend for the good of all of us."

Transitioning

Abby Marks-Beale relates an amusing anecdote about technology resistance. "Whenever I went to my local gas station to fill up, the touch screen would invite me to 'Request a speed pass.' Repeatedly, I touched, 'No, thank you.' I was thinking, 'What's that? It's unknown, too scary. I don't need that,' and so on.

"One day I pulled in to refill and watched in amazement as the woman at the pumps ahead of me waved a small cylinder on her key chain over what must have been some kind of infrared eye, filled her tank, and drove away. She never had to open her wallet or pay the attendant inside or swipe a credit card.

"Seeing is believing! I touched 'Send me the pass,' and have been hooked on the convenience ever since."

Rai Cockfield of IBM says, "To adopt technology, the need must exceed the difficulty of adoption," which means if you want it badly enough, you'll do it. True enough, but transitioning to new technologies—hardware and software—is a big issue for many people.

By now, you are very aware of the benefits of e-organization. But I would be dishonest if I didn't admit that there are hidden costs, such as the time that you have to spend reading manuals, practicing buttons, styluses, and commands, managing batteries, synchronizing, and backing up. As one friend vented to me, "I have a business to run and a family to support. I don't have time to stop what I'm doing and learn all I have to know to do this!"

"Hold on," I replied. "I never said, 'Stop what you're doing.' I said, 'Write down your goal, list the smaller bites, and schedule those bites into your life *one at a time* until you get the job done. Along the way, get good advice and delegate all you can.' " And now the last and most important requirement: Make yourself accountable to someone else.

Possible steps for learning and implementing new technology include:

- Purchase and read a tutorial on CD-ROM.
- Take a continuing-ed class.
- Take a class on-line.
- Hire an e-coach to teach you.

If you wish to get rid of your paper Rolodex once and for all, but wonder how you're going to find the time to enter all your contacts into your electronic address book, you have only a few options:

- Set aside, say, thirty minutes a day for doing data entry yourself.

- Burrow in for a whole day on the weekend to get the job done.
- Hire someone, say, a teenager after school, to do the data entry.

Moving from a paper-based, or even a computer, calendar to a PDA is not difficult. One day soon after receiving my PDA, I simply began putting all future appointments in my PDA calendar. It was blissfully easy, especially the "repeat" function, which allows me to have appointments recur every day, weekly, biweekly, monthly, and so on into infinity. I never again have to purchase a paper calendar and copy onto many pages recurring meetings, family birthdays, or other important events. For a while, my paper calendar accompanied me as a backup, but after only a few weeks I was confident and convinced—and the paper version was history.

Many people first become skilled at new systems in the workplace. When they experience their timesaving and e-organizing value, they want to bring them home to their nonwork lives. Often they can't afford, or get a license for, the same hardware and software, so they buy and install something similar. Again, they do it at work because they have to. Therefore, they will have to set up similar accountability for at home. To ensure that you will learn and implement your new technology, make sure that you set appropriate deadlines in your electronic calendar and then announce your intentions to another person who will cheer you when you're successful and jeer you when you fall short.

Ensure Compliance

In between meetings with your Mastermind Group, or informal sessions with your accountability buddy (sometimes called a "goal buddy"), here are some techniques to help ensure you'll get your home systems up and running:

- Plan to enjoy a reward following completion of the task. If the task seems very onerous, or the satisfaction you'll receive from completing it won't be enough to motivate you, set up an enticing reward to come after its conclusion.
- Is the job too big? Make sure you've broken down your elephant into the smallest possible bites.
- Have you set a deadline? This may seem obvious to users of electronic calendars, but if all you read on your calendar next Sunday is "clean out the garage," you need to see an *end time*, followed by your reward.
- Delegate the work—even barter if you can't afford to pay.

Jane Pollak says emphatically, "It's not an option to change what I've planned to accomplish today. Sometimes it's painful and I'm scared, but I do it anyway."

Not everyone is as successful as Jane is at harnessing his own internal accountability. "People can be highly motivated and still sabotage their good intentions," says Midé Wilkey. "Two behaviors usually come into play here: personal attitudes, including your 'self-talk,' and your interpersonal skills."

However, Midé insists that his coaching clients are able to sustain their motivation, and seldom undermine their goals, because those goals are aligned with their personal mission, which is based on their values. "If what you want to accomplish fits in with the larger picture for how you want your life to go, it's much easier to make the sacrifices necessary," he maintains.

Finding Focus in a Fog

I talk to a large number of people who confide that they feel adrift, without a plan, and lacking any vision of where they want to be. Often these individuals are very busy—indeed, it is often their busyness that clouds their vision and renders them too distracted, or too exhausted, to examine their bigger picture. Other temporarily aimless individuals are consultants and entrepreneurs, who are, as my flamboyant actress friend puts it, "between pictures"—that is, between large projects that energize their creative juices and provide focus. Perhaps the affliction can best be summed up by a participant in one of my workshops: "My goal is to have a goal," she said. And *that* is a very legitimate goal.

Very practical, action-oriented antidotes to the affliction can be found in the *lifetime learning habits*:

- Read, on-line and off-. Find out what interesting things people are doing.
- View and try demos. Try out what some people are doing.
- Shop, but don't buy . . . yet. Go in person. Touch and feel what people are doing.
- Ask, ask, ask. Talk to people about what they love, what they feel passionate about.
- Share tips with colleagues. Reveal your findings and other ideas with friends and mentors.

You can also shorten, and minimize the severity of, the time you spend directionless by following the steps to getting e-organized:

1. Use technology to save time. Sharpen your skills, learn some new shortcuts, and enjoy your sense of accomplishment.
2. Have a system for processing and storing documents. As you learn and pursue other possible opportunities, keep track of them in an organized way so you can retrieve what you learn when you need it.
3. Write down your goals and the specific timetables for accomplishing them.
4. Practice timesaving communication strategies. Don't let increased electronic access divert you from your goals. Use it to protect the time you've set aside to work on them.
5. Have a system for personal accountability—a Mastermind Group, a goal buddy, a friend—who will hold you responsible for finding a new focus.

The Challenge to Disconnect

It is not new news that, thanks to advances in mobile communications, more and more people are telecommuting. It is no longer necessary to do your work only at your workplace. Absent commuting and workplace distractions, employees can often be more focused and productive. Likewise, these same advances allow workers to keep in closer touch with family and loved ones when they're away from home.

Technology's detractors argue that, instead of bringing more freedom, technology has increased the pressure to do more in less time and produced a blurring of work and home life. I don't buy that. For me, and for those who strive to be more e-organized, technology has given me more options throughout my day and week. Years ago I went to work and did nothing but work, then came home and enjoyed personal time. One line between work and free time was firmly drawn. Today I still draw clear lines between work and play but have the freedom to move in and out of those spheres with more flexibility. Now I can choose to read and answer e-mail in the evening or exercise with a friend in the middle of the afternoon. I often take a two-day "weekend" in the middle of the week and catch up on work demands straight through Saturday and Sunday, thanks to my 24/7 connectivity.

As I wrote in chapter 4, I think the real challenge presented by all the opportunities to stay connected is in deciding when to *disconnect*. And the importance of being disconnected cannot be disputed.

"Things happen when we are alone in our heads," wrote James Gleick in the *New York Times Magazine*, "and they are things we can't live without: contemplation, reflection, focus." The corporate CEOs I have interviewed confirm this when they confess that they get new ideas on their sailboats, while climbing mountains, or dangling a fishing line in a quiet, secluded lake.

Perhaps it all just comes down to an attitude—more options from technology or more pressure. I draw *my* conclusions from the testimonials of the converted.

"My stress level has been reduced by half since I purchased a CRM package and hired a geek to coach me and my staff," says Lorraine D., the interior decorator whose lack of organizing tools kept her feeling out of control. "We no longer waste time trying to remember what a client decided. The entire history of her decisions is on the computer, along with calendar reminders to check on deliveries and installations."

Frank and Anne E. purchased PDAs, and as they suspected, they're saving lots of time by syncing their calendars and contacts. They've also committed to coaching each other to maximize their investment. "We have a lot of friends who have just turned on their PDAs and are kind of stumbling along, not getting the full benefit," Anne says. "Frank and I have set aside one evening each week to teach the other what we've learned, share free software, practice shortcuts, and so on."

Jack M., the lonely bachelor, is enjoying a busy social life and conducted all his research on-line. "I never knew my area was so rich with things to do," he exclaims. "I've joined a cycling club, participated in several charity walks, and even found myself heading up a road rally for the Jaycees. And yes, I'm meeting some nice women." Go, Jack!

Paul S. is totally sold on his tickler file and his business card scanner. "I'm so much more productive now that I no longer waste time looking for lost papers, names—what have you. I've also hired my nephew to help with routine filing two afternoons a week. Eliminating my 'paper stress' has given me time to tackle more important to-dos I'd been putting off for months."

Cynthia S., with the help of a Mastermind Group for entrepreneurs, has learned how to disconnect and therefore achieve that important creative time that she so desperately needed. "I had to learn I am *not* 911," she says. "Members of my group were very sympathetic—as entrepreneurs, it's easy to fall into the trap of 'If I don't answer the phone, I'm missing a business opportunity.' In fact, if I don't do my work, I'll be out of business! And a unified messaging service is helping me keep in touch on *my* terms."

Each of these individuals has learned how to work smarter, not harder. They use technology to save time, reduce steps, keep track of details, simplify their lives, and even, like Jack M., to have fun. "I no longer feel overwhelmed," insists Steven L., who is joined by a chorus of other e-organized people who are proclaiming their reduced stress.

Ride the Wave!

Several years ago I attended a technology conference where I heard a prediction that one day soon I would be wearing the Internet around my neck. My immediate gut reaction was to turn away in disgust, hold my head in my hands, and grimace while my mind said, "It's too scary, too awful. I don't want to be there," and similar protests.

Soon after that conference, I made a decision to enroll in e-college and to practice lifetime learning habits. I'm no longer uncomfortable with that idea. The Internet is here, and for better or for worse, just like the computer, it has changed our lives. And a whole new branch of social science—pervasive computing—has emerged.

One thing is certain: "In the future, everybody is going to have some type of computer literacy and knowledge of the Internet," says Kip Smith, a Delta spokesperson. "It's a staple of life now, like the telephone became in the last century."

Yes, the technology tsunami is not going away, and I've decided to ride the wave.

Index

A

accountability, 5, 81, 139–42,
    144, 145, 147
  buddy, 145, 147
  groups, 141–42
action bites, 101
Active Desktop, 62, 116
address book, 29, 33, 35, 77
  data-sharing, 78
  electronic, 32, 77, 79, 93,
    143
  on pager, 44
advertising, 42, 114, 123
affordability, 27
agenda, 134, 135
all-in-one communications,
    125–26, 127
America Online (AOL), 114,
    118, 127
  instant messenger (AIM),
    121
antivirus software, 44, 71
applications suite, 77
appointments
  external, 106, 140
  internal, 106, 140
  regular, 56, 74, 81
Asmar, Charles, 67, 112
autofocus, 50
automated backup, 69

B

backup, 33, 66–69
  automated, 69
  memory, 44
  online, 67
  system, 33, 54, 66–67, 69
bartering, 22, 145
beaming, 44, 77
Better Business Bureau, 72
bills, 39, 58, 59, 95
Bisset, Drew, 40
blind copy, 117
Bliss, Edwin, 2
bookmarks, 62, 63
brainstorming, 91–105, 134
  bite-size, 92, 93, 97, 100,
    101, 103
Brenner, Scott, 63

broadband, 68, 69, 71
browser, 61, 73
buckets of minutes, 39
buddy list, 121
built-in flash, 50
bundling functions, 17, 48
business cards, 78
Buzan, Tony, 96

C

cable modem, 68
cache, clearing, 121
call forwarding, 39, 42
call waiting, 39
caller ID, 39, 123
card scanner, 78
Carlson, Jeff, 33, 34, 68
Castenada, John, 38
CD-R (compact disk
　　recordable), 66
CD-RW (compact disk
　　rewritable), 66
cell phones, *see* mobile
　　phones
Chamber of Commerce, 42
clutter, 56, 76, 81
Cockfield, Rai, 143
combination devices, 28,
　　47–48
compact disk, 66
Competitive Edge Magazine,
　　55
Consumer Reports, 49
continuing education, 19, 23,
　　99, 143
Corel, 24
CRM (customer relationship

management), 56, 78, 79,
　　80–81, 93, 102, 107

D

data-sharing address book,
　　78
Day Runners, 3
Day-Timers, 3
dead zones, 40
deadlines, 108
decision making, 81, 82
delegating, 111, 130–32, 133,
　　145
desktop organizers, 60, 61
digital
　　cameras, 2, 17, 28, 31, 47,
　　　48–53
　　dictation, 128
　　highlighters, 2
　　tape drives, 67
　　video camera, 47
Direct Mail Association, 56
Direct Marketing Association,
　　122
distribution list, 113
documents
　　electronic, 54, 55, 58, 61, 63,
　　　69, 73
　　estate planning documents,
　　　59, 65
　　management, 60, 139, 147
　　paper, 55, 58, 63, 64, 74,
　　　139
　　reader, 34
DragStrip, 61
DSL (digital subscriber line),
　　68, 70, 103

dual band, 36
DVD (digital video disk)
    player, 48

E

e-audit, 6, 9–13
e-coach, 6, 137, 143
e-college, 7, 22, 150
e-jokes, 57, 113
e-mail, 16, 29, 36, 43, 44, 46,
    52, 57, 66, 71, 79, 112,
    115, 125, 135
  addresses, 29, 78, 79, 120
  automatic signature, 115
  autoresponders, 116
  blind copy function, 117
  cache, 121
  dictating, 128–29
  etiquette, 117, 122
  filters, 114
  forwarding, 39
  greetings, 26
  junk, 112
  organizing, 112–13
  productivity, 112–22
  subject line, 116
  suppliers, 119, 120
e-tailers, 72, 73, 113
effective communicators, 111,
    133
electronic
  address book, 32, 77, 79, 93,
    143
  calendar, 29, 32, 44, 56, 75,
    79, 81, 106, 107, 144
  documents, 54, 55, 58, 61,
    63, 69, 73

greetings, 118
  organizing tools, 61, 78, 106
  schedule, 80
Electronic Signature law, 72
encryption, 68
equipment protection plan,
    37, 46
estate planning documents,
    59, 65
Excel, 24, 33
executive coaching, 141
expiration date, 64, 116
external appointments, 106,
    140

F

fax, 17, 46, 95, 117, 125, 126,
    132
FCC (Federal Communications
    Commission), 40
filing system, 58–59, 76
Filofax, 3
FinderKeeper, 61
firewall, 69, 70, 103
Fisher, Brad, 84, 139
Fleming, Peter, 129
floppy disks, 49, 65, 66
Franklin Planners, 3

G

Gartner Group, 13
*Getting Organized: The Easy
    Way to Put Your Life in
    Order* (Winston), 3, 55
Gilbreth, Frank, 2
Gleick, James, 148

global messaging, 43
goal-setting requirements,
     88–91
Guernsey, Lisa, 85

H
hackers, 69, 71
halfway house (for clutter),
     82
handheld organizers, 2, 30.
     See also PDAs.
hardcopy papers, 55, 64, 75
help screens, 17, 21, 84
Hemphill, Barbara, 60
hoaxes, 71
home network, 19, 67
Hotmail, 120
http://calendar.yahoo.com,
     33
http://consumer.usa.canon.
     com/index.shtml, 17
http://cruisewithme.com/
     help, 20
http://dir.yahoo.com/
     Business_and_Economy/
     Shopping_and_Services/
     Communication_and_
     Information_
     Management/Internet_
     and_World_Wide_Web/
     Personal_Information_
     Management/Photo_
     Albums/, 51
http://download.cnet.com, 34
http://equip.zdnet.com, 38
http://greetings.yahoo.com,
     119

http://groups.yahoo.com/
     local/news.html, 119
http://messenger.msn.com,
     121
http://messenger.yahoo.com,
     121
http://motorola.com/MIMS/
     MSPG/Products/
     Two-Way/timeport_
     p935/, 43
http://news.com.com/
     2001-12.0.html?-tag=
     hd_ts, 23
http://web.icq.com, 121
http://www.aladdinsys.com/
     dragstrip/winindex.html,
     61
http://www.dailyedeals.com/
     free_internet/free_isp.
     htm, 120
http://www.lginfocomm.com/
     home/LGI300W_
     phone.asp, 47
http://www.newdream.org/
     junkmail/step1.html, 56
http://www.simplifythe-
     holidays.org, 119
http://www.state.ct.us/dcp/
     nocall.htm, 123

I
image-editing tools, 51
inbox, 57, 58, 75, 125, 126
infrared transfer, 44, 77
instant messaging, 121–22
internal appointments, 106,
     140

Internet, 3, 18, 113, 150
  backup, 67
  broadband, 102–3
  connections, 19
  Explorer, 121
  innovations, 35
  learning about, 24
  mobile phones and, 36, 47
  pagers and, 45, 46
  PDAs and, 29
  photo-sharing, 49, 50, 52
  research, 84, 93, 95
  restrictions (for young
    children), 70
  security, 69–73, 121
  storage space, 68
  telephony, 95
  watchdogs, 113
  wireless, 32, 39
Internet Telephony, 95
interoperability, 27, 52, 122
investment records, 63, 65
invisible Web, 85
IP (Internet protocol), 95
ISP (Internet service
    provider), 19, 119, 120

J
Jaz drive, 67
junk mail, 56

K
Kabak, Joanne, 71, 72
Kehlenbeck, Vickery, 71
key codes, 65
keywords, 60

L
Lakein, Alan, 2
Laliberté, Susan, 57
land stations, 40
land-line phones, 40
leading by example, 116–22
lifetime learning habits,
    22–26, 31, 86, 94, 103,
    111, 138, 146, 150
long-distance charges, 38–39,
    40
long-term goals, 96–100
Lotus software products, 24,
    79

M
Mac users, 61
Marks-Beale, Abby, 57, 83,
    116–17, 142
Mastermind Group, 141–42,
    145, 147
meetings, 110, 119, 133–36,
    141
megapixels, 50
memory backup, 44
memory card, 49
Microsoft
    Active Desktop, 62, 116
    Excel, 24, 33
    Hotmail, 120
    Internet Explorer, 121
    Outlook, 79, 112, 119
    Word, 24, 33, 51, 64
mind mapping, 96–97, 100
mobile phones, 2, 17, 27–28,
    35–43, 44, 47, 48, 53, 79,
    125

modem card, 37
Morgan, Rebecca, 23
MP3 players, 2, 47
My Documents folder, 61

N
National Association of
    Professional Organizers,
    3
no-call list, 123
Norton Internet Security
    Family Edition, 70

O
O'Farrell, Allen, 51
on-line
    backup, 67
    banking, 71, 72
    courses, 23–24
    investing, 71, 72
    security, 71–72
    shopping, 38, 71, 73
    solutions, 20
    storage, 52
    technology news, 23
    transactions, 72
operating systems, 34, 61
outgoing voicemail
    instructions, 124
Outlook, 79, 112, 119

P
pagers, 27–28, 43–47, 48, 53
paging service, 46
Paine, Lee, 49

Pakman, David, 68
Palm, Inc., 3
*Palm Organizers Visual
    Quickstart Guide*
    (Carlson), 33
Palm OS, 30, 34, 47
palmtop organizers, *see* PDAs
Pankratz, Christopher, 121
panorama mode, 50
paper
    documents, 55, 58, 63, 64,
        74, 139
    management software, 60
    piles of, 54, 55, 56, 75,
        81–84
password protection, 44, 65,
    67
PDAs, 3, 29–35, 48, 53, 75,
    107, 125, 129
    advances in, 17, 125
    combination devices, 47
    data transfer, 44, 77–78, 79
    portability, 27–28, 77
    security, 68
    transition to, 144
    Web-enabled, 78
phone support, 21–22
photo-sharing, 50–51
PICs (personal interactive
    communicators), 43. *See
    also* two-way pagers.
PIM (personal information
    management), 78, 79, 93,
    106
PIN (personal identification
    number) codes, 65, 72
Pocket PC OS, 30
Pocket PCs, *see* PDAs

Pocket Quicken, 29
Pollak, Jane, 7, 96–97, 105, 145
pop-up dialog box, 121
Popular Photography, 49
portability, 26–27, 36, 68, 77
priorities, 58, 116, 130, 132
privacy, 44, 69–73, 121
    policy, 71, 113
product comparison, 38, 49
product cycle, 16, 27, 48
productivity, 16, 28, 32, 39, 40, 42, 47, 48, 58, 111
    e-mail, 112–22
    telephone, 122–29
professional organizer, 57, 64
purging files, 64

R

reading team, 83
rechargeable battery, 42, 45, 50
recycling bin, 57, 82, 83
reduced stress, 2, 148
regular appointments, 56, 74, 81
resellers, 41
reverse delegation, 130
roaming, 40, 46
Rolodex, 77, 78, 93, 143
router, 70

S

safe-deposit box, 60, 64, 65
satellite, 40, 43
scanner, 17, 60, 65, 78

Scherer, Judy, 55
Schor, Juliet B., 3
search directories, 84
search engines, 21, 67, 84, 85
secure transaction, 71
security, 65, 68, 69–73, 120–21
service contract, 21, 39–40, 46
service plans, 25, 28, 38, 40–41, 44, 46, 128
short-term goals, 93, 96
shortcuts, 61
signatures, 72, 115
smart keyboards, 2
snail mail, 57, 115
Social Security number, 72
software registration numbers, 65
software tutorials, 21
spam, 112, 114
speech recognition software, 3, 104, 128, 129
Speech Technology Magazine, 129
spot metering, 50
Start Menu, 61
storage space, 64, 66, 68
subscription services, 23
synchronization, 28, 79

T

t-coach, 20, 41, 95
tape drive, 67
tech (technical) support, 7, 18, 19, 20–22, 35, 51
technology advisor, 6, 17, 18, 66, 69

technology resistance, 142–43
telecommunications advisor, 20, 46
telecommunications consultant, 41–42, 123
telemarketing calls, 122
telephone tag, 123
text messaging, 39, 46
thinking bites, 101
three-way conference calling, 39
tickler file, 56, 74, 75–81
time and motion studies, 2
time management, 2, 7, 108–9, 111, 136, 139
to-do list, 29, 31, 33, 69, 79, 106, 107
toll-free message service, 46
TRAF, 55
transitioning, 34–35, 142–44
triband, 37
TRUSTe, 72
tsunami, 2, 5, 150
tutorials, 21, 23
twenty-four/seven (24/7) access, 22, 67, 148
two-way pagers, 43–47
two-way radio, 2, 37

U

unified messaging service, 125–26, 127, 137, 149–50
Universal Wireless Communications Consortium, 40
upgrade, 18, 31

URL (uniform resource locator), 42, 62, 72

V

video conferencing, 133
viewfinder, 50
virtual assistants, 132–33
virtual hard drives, 67
viruses, 71
voice
    command, 39
    mail, 39, 42, 123–24
    portals, 127
    recognition, 127

W

Web
    backup services, 67
    browsers, 46, 62, 73
    camera, 61
Web-enabled, 28, 42, 47, 78, 120
Web sites, 19, 50, 101, 113
    combination devices, 47
    digital cameras, 49
    e-greetings, 119
    e-mail, free, 120
    employment, 101
    establishing, 19, 96
    financial, 85
    instant messaging tools, 121
    ISPs, 120
    internet telephony, 95–96
    mobile phones, 38, 41
    on-line courses, 23–24

pagers, 43, 45
PDAs, 32–34
photo-sharing, 51
security, 70, 71
storage space, 68
tech support, 20–21
technology news, 23
telephone-based portals,
127
weeding out, 74
Welkovich, Stuart, 64
White, Steve, 112
Wilkey, Midé, 88, 91, 109, 145
Windows 98, 61, 69
Windows CE, 34
Winston, Stephanie, 2, 55
wireless Internet, 31, 39
wireless modem, 37
Word, 24, 33, 51, 64
written goals, 139
www.1onlinegreetingcards.
com, 119
www.32678.com/bill/palmos/
cspotrun, 34
www.4cellphones.com, 38
www.act.com, 78, 79
www.actpage.com, 45
www.adobe.com, 51
www.allexperts.com, 20
www.alphasmart.com, 2
www.altavista.com, 84
www.amazon.com, 119
www.aol.com, 121, 127
www.aportis.com. 33
www.askdrtech.com, 21
www.assistu.com, 132
www.avantgo.com, 33, 120
www.backup.net, 67

www.bhphotovideo.com, 49
www.blackberry.net, 43
www.blink.com, 42
www.bloomberg.com/bbn.
technology.html, 23
www.bluemountain.com, 119
www.buycrzone.com, 30, 41,
45
www.callserve.com, 95
www.callwave.com, 124
www.cardscan.com, 78
www.cbstelecom.com, 38
www.ccaii.com, 121
www.cellmania.com, 41
www.clubphoto.com, 51
www.cnet.com, 30, 41
www.compedgemag.com, 55
www.completeplanet.com, 85
www.computers4sure.com,
30, 49
www.connected.com, 67
www.daggerware.com, 34
www.dataviz.com, 33
www.dialpad.com, 96
www.dotphoto.com, 51
www.driveway.com, 68
www.egrabber.com, 79
www.elsware.com, 61
www.emailman.com, 122
www.epeople.com, 20
www.eshop.com, 38, 45
www.everythingemail.com,
122
www.evite.com, 119
www.excite.com, 21, 84, 120
www.expertcity.com, 20
www.financialengines.com, 85
www.financialfind.com, 85

www.fly.faa.gov, 62
www.freediskspace.com, 68
www.freedrive.com 68
www.freeskills.com, 24
www.freshaddress.com, 78
www.fusionone.com, 33
www.gadgetguru.com, 45
www.gator.com, 73
www.go.com, 21, 84
www.google.com, 21
www.groupcards.com, 119
www.growthcommunications.
    com, 112
www.hallmark.com, 119
www.handango.com, 32, 34
www.help.com, 20
www.helptalk.com, 20
www.heyanita.com, 127
www.highestrank.com, 67,
    112
www.hotbot.lycos.com, 84
www.iambic.com, 34
www.iconnecthere.com, 96
www.idg.net, 23
www.ilor.com, 85
www.imira.com, 51
www.internet101.org, 24
www.internettelephony.com,
    95
www.iomega.com, 66
www.isilo.com, 34
www.ivaa.org, 132
www.janepollak.com, 7, 96
www.junglemate.com, 78
www.kaylon.com/power.html,
    63
www.kodak.com/go/mc3, 47
www.kyocera.com, 47

www.landware.com, 29
www.learnthenet.com, 24, 114
www.linksys.com, 70
www.lowermybills.com, 38
www.lycos.com, 120
www.mcafee.com, 71
www.mcafee-at-home.com, 70
www.mediaring.com, 96
www.memoware.com, 32
www.microsoft.com, 51
www.mindmapper.com, 97
www.mobilegeneration.com,
    32
www.money-rates.com, 85
www.morningstar.com, 85
www.motorola.com/
    accompli009.com, 47
www.myhelpdesk.com, 21
www.myplay.com, 68
www.napo.net, 3
www.necoffee.com, 33
www.net2phone.com, 96
www.netforbeginners.about.
    com, 24
www.netvoice.com, 96
www.networkice.com, 70
www.netzero.com, 120
www.onstar.com, 127
www.onstream.com, 67
www.openwave.com, 79
www.outpost.com, 30
www.pagoo.com, 124
www.palm.com/products/
    compatible.html, 32
www.palmgear.com, 34
www.pandasoftware.com, 71
www.pcshowandtell.com, 20,
    23

www.pdajd.com, 34
www.pdastreet.com, 32
www.pockeydrives.com, 67
www.point.com, 38, 41
www.productivityconsultants.
  com, 60
www.protonic.com, 33
www.quickaid.com, 62
www.quicken.com, 29
www.rc.com, 71
www.samsungusa.com, 17
www.searchenginewatch.com,
  85
www.simulring.com, 42, 125
www.smartmoney.com, 85
www.SNPower.com, 42
www.sourcevelocity.com, 70
www.speechtek.com, 129
www.staffcentrix.com, 133
www.symantec.com, 70, 71
www.synsolutions.com, 34
www.techknow-how.com, 21
www.tellme.com, 127
www.thecamerazone.com, 49
www.thefetcher.com, 116
www.the-reading-edge.com,
  57, 83, 116

www.tinysoftware.com, 70
www.tmcnet.com, 95
www.tradetek.com, 85
www.unified-messaging.com,
  125
www.ureach.com, 125
www.vindigo.com, 34
www.visto.com, 51
www.voicecom.com, 125
www.weather.com, 62
www.wesync.com, 107
www.wirelessadvisor.com, 41
www.worldtimeserver.com,
  62
www.worldwidelearn.com,
  24
www.xdrive.com, 68
www.yahoo.com, 21, 84
www.zdnet.com/smartplanet/,
  24
www.zonealarm.com, 70
www.zoskware.com, 34

Z

Zip drive, 66
zoom lens, 50

Lucy H. Hedrick is the author of *Five Days to an Organized Life* (Dell, 1990), *365 Ways to Save Time* (William Morrow, 1992), *365 Ways to Save Time with Kids* (William Morrow, 1993), and *365 Ways to Save Money* (William Morrow, 1994). These four titles have sold more than 200,000 copies and been translated into eight languages.

Lucy has had a distinguished career in communications, training, and sales. She parlayed the contents of her four bestselling books on saving time and money into corporate training seminars and work as a product spokesperson. She has traversed the country on behalf of Dayton-Hudson, Kraft General Foods, Filofax, Black & Decker, and Quaker Oats.

As Founder and President of Hedrick Communications, Lucy is a public relations consultant to entrepreneurs and nonprofit organizations. In addition, she coaches authors on how to write nonfiction book proposals.

From 1995 to 1999, she worked at InfoEdge, Inc., a technology publishing and marketing company in Stamford, CT. Her first position was managing editor, in which she directed the publication of more than thirty book-length technology reports, after which she was promoted to sales manager.

Lucy earned her B.A. from Goucher College. She serves on the board of Perrot Memorial Library, Old Greenwich, and the Business Advisory Committee of Greenwich Library.

Please visit her Web site at http://www.lucyhedrick.com.